BASIC TECHNIQUES OF GO

by Haruyama Isamu 9-dan

and

Nagahara Yoshiaki 6-dan

edited by

Richard Bozulich

Ishi Press
San Jose, London, Tokyo

Pulished by
The Ishi Press, Inc.
CPO Box 2126
Tokyo, Japan

In North America, this book may be ordered from:
Ishi Press International
76 Bonaventura Drive
San Jose, CA
USA 95134

In Europe or the U.K., order from:
Ishi Press International
20 Bruges Place
London NW1 0TE, U.K.

ISBN 4-87187-002-2

First printing February 1969
Second Edition January 1973
Eighth Printing August 1987
Third edition May 1992
Printed in Japan

Contents

Preface to the Third Edition

This book is written for players who know the rules and the most elementary tactics and wish to reach expert strength. It assumes that the reader has read one of the Ishi Press beginner books such as *Introduction to Go*, *The Magic of Go*, or *Go for Beginners*.

The text of this edition has been completely rewritten, although the diagrams (and content) are nearly the same as those in the second edition. The only major change has been the up-dating of an old *joseki* by Rob van Zeijst, which appears in the appendix. In addition, the order of the chapters has been changed: what is now Chapter Five, Tesuji, was Chapter One in the previous two editions. In addition, a number of errors have been corrected.

In the first two editions, Japanese terms were used throughout the book. In this edition, I have eliminated almost all these terms, retaining only the most essential ones such as *atari*, *sente*, *gote*, etc. These terms are defined in the glossary at the beginning. I believe this change will make this book more accessible to all beginning players.

The three main areas of go are covered in this book: the opening, the middle game, and the endgame. The emphasis in the opening sections is on handicap go. Since beginners plays most of their games with handicaps, they will have ample opportunity to adopt the strategies described in this book. It is hoped that these strategies will help them win most of their high-handicap games.

Richard Bozulich
April, 1992

Technical Terms

Go has a number of technical terms which refer to concepts basic to the understanding of its tactics and strategies. Some of these terms are in Japanese have no good English equivalents, the reader should simply learn what is meant by them and add these words to his go vocabulary. Henceforth, these terms will be used just as if they were English words.

Atari

Atari is a threat to capture a stone or a group of stones on the next move. *Diagrams 1a to 1c* is an example. In *Dia. 1a*, the white stone is in *atari*, since Black can capture it on the next move by playing at 'a'. White could escape by extending to the point 'a' himself. If White doesn't play at 'a', Black could capture by playing 1 in *Dia. 1b*. The result of this capture is shown in *Dia. 1c*. When one player puts an opponent's stone or stones in *atari*, he will often announce this by saying 'atari' (although this isn't required), just as one announces 'check' in chess.

Dia. 1a

Dia. 1b

Dia. 1c

Sente and Gote

A move is called *sente* if it creates a threat so large that the other player cannot avoid responding to it. *Gote* is the opposite: it is a move which is defends a position and the other player need not respond to it. (Note that many gote moves have some aggressive potential and are not completely defensive.) *Dia. 2* is an example:

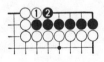

Dia. 2

White 1 is sente. Black must answer it by playing 2. If Black omits this move, White will play at 2 and the black stones will die. On the other hand, Black 2 is gote. It only defends the stones in the corner and creates no threats. White can now play elsewhere.

Fuseki

The *fuseki* is the opening stage of the game in which the two players map out there prospective territories. It is usually defined as lasting until the first fight begins. In this book we will use the English word 'opening' to refer to the *fuseki*.

Joseki

A *joseki* is a set sequence which are the best moves for each side. Joseki usually take place in the corners, although they can also occur on the side; some even involve a whole side of the board. They usually occur in the opening stages of the game.

Ko

One of the rules of go states the no previous board position may be recreated. This rule prevents endlessly repetitive situations from occuring.

Dia. 3

Diagram 3 shows an example. If Black captures the marked stone with 1, then White recaptures the marked stone, Black again recaptures, etc., we would have an endlessly repetitive situation. The *ko* rule prevents this from happening. After Black captures at 1, White must play on a point other than where the marked stone was. If Black doesn't connect at the point where the marked stone is with move 3, then White can recapture the black stone at 1.

Ladder

A 'ladder' is a method of capturing stones which results in a pattern resembling the steps of a ladder tilted diagonally. *Diagram 4* below is an example.

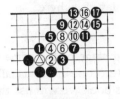

Dia. 4

Black 1 catches the marked white stone in a ladder. If White resists, Black will drive him to the edge of the board and capture all his stones with 17. If White had a stone in the vicinity of 10 before Black played 1, the ladder would not work and Black's efforts would end in failure. Such a stone is called a ladder-breaker. When you are thinking about capturing a stones with this tactic, close attention must be paid to all stones in the line of the projected ladder.

Chapter One

Principles of Even-Game Openings

a) The Opening Moves

In the opening both players should aim at occupying the corners because it is easier to construct territory there. Moreover, a stone in the corner can be easily defended.

Dia. 1 (Six stones, nine points)

Black's six stones in the corner surround nine points of territory.

Dia. 2 (Nine stones, nine points)

For Black to get nine points on the side, he needs nine stones. Now try taking nine points in the center. You will find that twelve stones are necessary. These diagrams illustrate a basic principle of the opening: 'Play first in the corners, then on the sides, and finally in the center.'

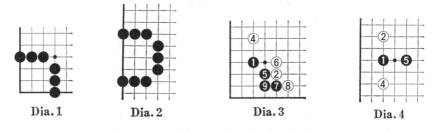

Dia. 1   Dia. 2   Dia. 3   Dia. 4

Dia. 3 (It's easy to defend the corner)

This diagram shows that a stone in the corner can be easily defended. Black has played 1 in the corner, and White attacks it with 2. If Black ignores this move and plays 3 elsewhere, letting White attack again with 4, Black can still play the sequence to 9. Black's stones in the corner are now secure and White has no viable way to attack them. Note that this way of playing is a bit inelegant; it is given only for the purpose of illustration.

Dia. 4 (Defense on the side is harder)

If Black plays a stone on the side with 1, letting White have two moves with 2 and 4 leaves the black stone without a base. Black's only recourse is to jump into the center with 5. Without the option of securing a base on the side, these two black stones could become a burden on Black.

Dia. 5 (The usual opening corner moves)

There are five corner points where the first move is usually played: the 3–4 point at 'a', the 3–3 point at 'b', the star point (the 4–4 point) at 'c', the 5–3 point at 'd' and the 5–4 point at 'e'. Each of these moves has a different strategic aim.

Dia. 6 (The 3–4 point)

A black stone on the 3–4 point is easily defended, as we saw in *Dia. 3* above. The stability of a stone on this point enables Black to answer a white approach move at 2 (or 'a') with a pincer at any of the points 'b', 'c', 'd', 'e' or 'f'. If White neglects to play an approach move, Black could enclose the corner by playing at 2 (or 'a') himself, taking a profit there. Corner enclosures will be studied in the next section.

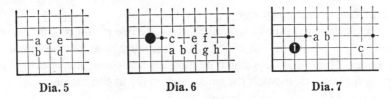

Dia. 5   **Dia. 6**   **Dia. 7**

Dia. 7 (The 3–3 point)

When Black plays a stone at the 3–3 point, he intends to secure the corner with one move. If White doesn't attack this stone, Black can make a corner enclosure at 'a' or 'b', or extend to 'c' depending on the situation.

Dia. 8 (The shoulder hit)

The shoulder hit of White 1 is a severe attack. The moves to White 5 are a typical exchange. Black secures the corner, while White gets outside influence.

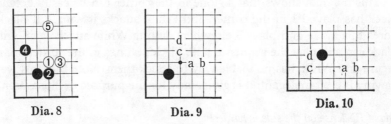

Dia. 8   **Dia. 9**   **Dia. 10**

Dia. 9 (Other ways White can attack)

Besides the shoulder hit of White 1 in *Dia. 8*, White can also attack the 3–3 point stone with an approach move at 'a' or 'b'. If White 'a', Black 'c' is the usually reply; if White 'b', Black 'c' and 'd' are both possible.

Dia. 10 (The star point)

The strategy of the star point is just the opposite to that of the 3–3 point. When Black plays 1 on the star point, he is not concerned with territory; rather, he wishes to use this stone to get influence on the outside. That's why it's not a good idea for Black to make a corner enclosure at 'a' or 'b', since this kind of move doesn't secure the corner — White can still invade at 'c' and live. To secure the corner, Black needs an additional move at 'd'. However, using three moves to enclose a corner is a bit slow. This is contrary to the strategy of playing on the star point, which is quick development.

Dia. 11 (Invading the corner)

When Black plays on the star point, he should not worry about a white invasion at the 3–3 point. Rather, he should extend to 1 (or even as far as 'a', depending on the situation) and hope White invades. Look at the result when White invades at 2. Black blocks at 3 and the moves to 13 naturally follow. White has taken the corner while Black has magnificent thickness. The black stone at 1 is on a very good point (in this case, 'a' would be even better). White has gained about 10 points in the corner, but the value of Black's outside thickness is far greater.

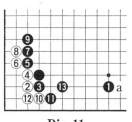

Dia. 11

Dia. 12

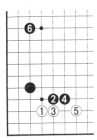

Dia. 13

Dia. 12 (The 5–3 point))

When Black plays 1 at the 5–3 point, his intention here is to emphasize the side. The usual way for White to attack this stone is to play at 'a'. If White neglects to play this move, Black will occupy 'a' and make a corner enclosure.

Dia. 13 (Black expands the side)

Against White 1, Black's standard reply is to press at 2. Up to 5, White secures some area on the lower side, and Black extends to 6, expanding his area on the left side.

Dia. 14 (The 5–4 point)

A move on the 5–4 point emphasizes central influence. It is not as tight as the star point, since White has more leeway when he invades the corner at 'a'. Still, the 5–4 point is not inferior. If White neglects to play at 'a', Black will play there to make a corner enclosure.

Dia. 15 (White is confined to the corner)

This diagram shows how easy it is for Black to get central influence with the 5–4 point. When White plays 2, Black plays a knight's move with 3. After the moves to Black 7, White is confined to the corner, while Black dominates the center.

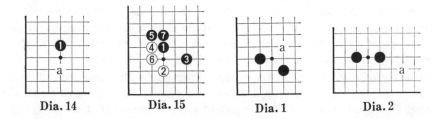

| Dia. 14 | Dia. 15 | Dia. 1 | Dia. 2 |

b) Corner enclosures

In the opening, it is quite common for one or both players to make corner enclosures. The advantages of enclosing a corner are: 1) it secures a profit in the corner; 2) it projects influence along the sides and into the center. We will study the three main types of corner enclosures.

Dia. 1 (The small-knight corner enclosure)

The small-knight enclosure shown here is very popular among professional players nowadays. It emphasizes corner territory, but its influence towards the center is not so strong, because of a weak point at 'a'.

Dia. 2 (The one-point corner enclosure)

In contrast to the corner enclosure in Dia. 1, the one-point enclosure is strong in the direction of the center. However, the corner territory is not as secure because of a possible white approach at 'a'.

Dia. 3 (The large-knight corner enclosure)

The large-knight enclosure is similar to the small-knight enclosure in that it emphasizes defense of the corner. But this defense is looser. White can wrest the corner away from Black by invading at 'a', 'b' or 'c'. Moreover, there is also an erasure move at 'd'.

Dia. 4 (Developing from a corner enclosure)

Since a corner enclosure exerts influence along the sides, the best way to use this influence is by making an extension. The correct direction is towards 1, perpendicular to the line of the enclosure stones. Later, Black can play at 'a', forming the boundary for a huge valley of territory.

Dia. 5 (The wrong direction)

Extending to Black 1 is the wrong direction. This move should be played only after Black has played 1 in *Dia. 4*, because White can easily invade at 'b' or 'c', even after Black has reinforced at 'a'. In *Dia. 4*, however, the best White can do after Black reinforces at 'a' is to make an erasing move at 'b', to which Black responds with 'c'. In addition, the scale of Black 'a' in *Dia. 4* is much larger than the scale of Black 'a' in *Dia. 5*. These same principles of extending from a corner enclosure also hold true for both the small-knight and large-knight corner enclosures.

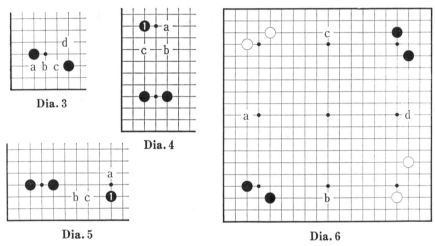

Dia. 3

Dia. 4

Dia. 5

Dia. 6

Dia. 6 (Priority of extension)

Black and White have each made two corner enclosures. Where is the key point for Black?

Since the black and white enclosures on the left side are facing each other along the line of their strongest influence, 'a' is the key point. Not only does it extend from the enclosure, it also limits the influence of the opponent's enclosure. The points 'b' and 'c' have almost the same value. If Black had already played at 'a', White would play 'b' next, since this would extend from his enclosure at the bottom right and limit the scope of Black's enclosure on the left. The point 'd' is the least important. An extension in this direction has the least value for either side.

Dia. 7 (The limit of an extension from a corner enclosure)

Black 1 is the furthest Black should extend from his enclosure. After extending to 1, he still has the possibility of another extension to 'a'. Extending as far as 'b' is not good. Black's stone is too close to the white enclosure, so he hasn't room to make a good extension.

Dia. 8 (The power of the one-point enclosure)

After Black plays the marked stone, White might invade with 1. Up to Black 8, White's invasion fails. He has no way of saving his four stones.

Dia. 9 (White escapes)

In contrast to *Dia. 8*, if Black has a small-knight enclosure, White's invasion will succeed. With the moves up to 5, he escapes into the center.

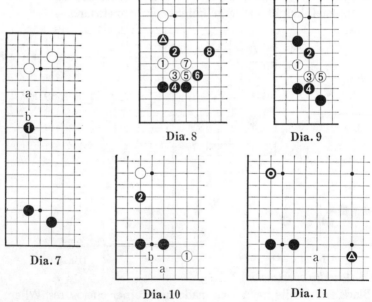

Dia. 8   Dia. 9

Dia. 7   Dia. 10   Dia. 11

Dia. 10 (Weakness in the corner)

The above examples show that the one-point enclosure exerts strong influence towards the center. However, since White can play at 1, this enclosure does not defend the corner so strongly. If Black extends to 2, White will aim at 'a', followed by Black 'b', Depending upon the situation, White might choose to play 'b' instead of 'a'.

Dia. 11 (Double-wing formation)

When Black has made a one-point enclosure, the extensions of the two marked stones are ideal. This shape is called a 'double-wing formation'. The reason why it's so good is that the marked stone on the left is a perfect extension from the strong side of the enclosure, while the marked stone at the bottom removes the weakness at 'a'. Moreover, the territory which Black is mapping out is very large.

Dia. 12 (Erasing Black's central influence)

However, when Black has a small-knight enclosure, the double-wing formation is not so effective. White can cap at 1, effectively erasing Black's central influence. The moves shown here are a common pattern. Instead of 12, Black could play 13, but the situation in the corner will become complicated. After 13, White will aim at attacking the marked black stone.

Dia. 13 (The diagonal move)

Against the cap of White 1, Black can reply with the diagonal move of 2 if he wants to secure territory on the lower side. The moves up to White 7 are one way of playing.

Dia. 14 (Sacrifice)

Even though White's stones in Dia. 13 seem thin, they are actually quite resilient. If Black pushes out and cuts with 1 and 3, White simply sacrifices three stones with the moves from 4 to 8. Black's 'ideal' extension (the marked stone) is now cut off and faces a strong white wall.

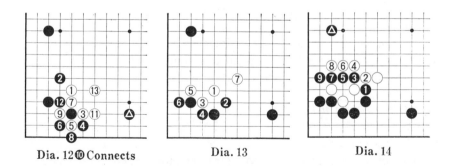

Dia. 12 ⑩ Connects   Dia. 13   Dia. 14

c) Approach Moves

A large advantage in one part of the board can be obtained by making a corner enclosure. Therefore, whenever possible, this should be prevented. The standard move used to do so is an approach move. Against the 3–4 point, there are four standard approach moves.

Dia. 1 (The small-knight approach)

Of all the approach moves, small-knight move of White 1 is the most severe. Not only does it prevent Black from securing territory in the corner, it also threatens to play at 'a' or 'b' next.

Dia. 2 (The diagonal attachment)

Black can certainly secure the corner by diagonally attaching at 2. The result to 5 is equal, but since Black played in the corner first, he should do better than this. A more aggressive style of playing is recommended.

Dia. 3 (The pincer)

The standard way of answering the approach move at 1 is with a pincer like 2. Other pincers, such as 'a', 'b', 'c', or 'd', can also be played. White responds by jumping to 3 and Black extends to 4, staking out territory on the side. This result is better for Black than *Dia.* 2: he has taken territory, while the two white stones are under attack.

Dia. 1   Dia. 2   Dia. 3

Dia. 4 (The diagonal response)

In certain circumstances, Black might also make the diagonal move of 2 against the approach of White 1. This is a good move, though not as severe as a pincer, because it's a bit slow. However, it gives Black a number of options: he can press at 'a' or extend to around 'b'. In addition, he can attack from the right with a pincer at 'c' or 'd'.

Dia. 5 (The one-space high approach)

If White is concerned about central influence, he will choose the one-space high approach of 1. Black can either answer with a pincer at 'a' or 'b' or attach at 'c' or 'd'. These are the most common. When Black wants to keep things peaceful, he may simply extend to 'e' or 'f',

Dia. 6 (Attaching)

Attaching at 2 is also a peaceful way of playing. After the moves to White 7, Black has a territory in the corner while White has developed along the side. In contrast to *Dia.* 2, this result is satisfactory for Black since his corner territory is larger than White's territory on the side.

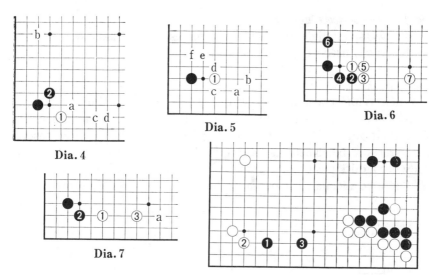

Dia. 4

Dia. 5

Dia. 6

Dia. 7

Dia. 8

Dia. 7 (The large-knight approach)

The large-knight approach of White 1 is a bit passive, because Black can respond with 2, thereby securing the corner. White must now extend to 3 to establish a base along the side. Black will now aim to attack the two white stones from the point 'a'. However, this result may not necessarily be bad; in some positions the large-knight approach may be a good move.

Dia. 8 (An ideal approach)

Considering White's thickness on the right, the large-knight approach of Black 1 is the best move available. If White defends the corner with 2, Black will extend to 3, nullifying White's thickness. Alternatively, for White to make a pincer around 3 would be too close to his thickness.

Dia. 9 (The wrong approach)

The small-knight approach of Black 1 allows White to utilize his thick position on the right to the maximum with the ideal pincer of 2.

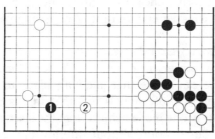

Dia. 9

Dia. 10 (The two-space high approach)

The two-space high approach of White 1 is also a passive way of playing. It is rarely used in professional play.

Dia. 11 ((White has failed)

When White plays 1, Black can play 2, 4, and 6, taking area in the corner almost as if he had made an enclosure. Since one of the reasons for playing an approach move is to prevent the formation of an enclosure, there seems to be something lacking in this move. However, if White already has a thick position towards the right, the wall made with the moves to 7 might be adequate compensation for the territory Black has taken.

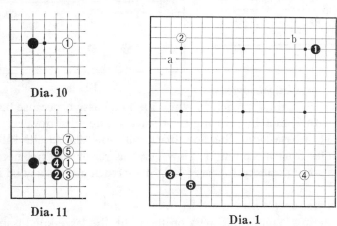

Dia. 10

Dia. 11

Dia. 1

d) Timing of Corner Enclosures, Approach Moves and Extensions

After stones have been placed in the four corners, a player must choose among making a corner enclosure, an approach move and an extension. The problems involved in this decision will be discussed in this section.

Dia. 1 (Corner enclosure of approach move?)

After the moves to 4, Black and White have occupied two corners each. Next, Black makes a corner enclosure with 5. The problem now is whether White should make a corner enclosure at 'a' or an approach move at 'b'.

Dia. 2 (Black makes two corner enclosures)

If White makes a corner enclosure at 1, Black will make another one at 2. Although no one can prove that allowing Black to make two corner enclosures is bad, most professionals feel that this is a passive way for White to play. White is one move behind from the start, so he shouldn't let Black take such a large profit without offering any resistance. Besides,

White has a stone on the star point in the lower right,so Black could take a third corner by invading at 'a'. In any case, if White plays 1, after Black makes a corner enclosure at 2, 3 is the next big point for White. This move develops his star point stone and limits Black's enclosure in the upper right corner. The moves from 3 to 6 follow naturally.

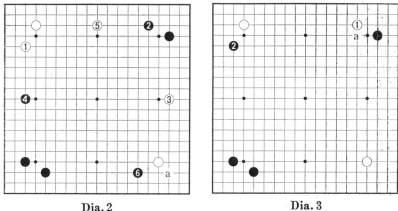

Dia. 2   Dia. 3

Dia. 3 (The approach move)

Playing the approach move at 1 or 'a' is White's best strategy. Black also plays an approach move at 2. This is a natural flow of stones. The focal point of the game is now on the left side.

Dia. 4 (Where should Black play his approach move?)

The sequence here is somewhat similar to *Dia. 1*, except that White 4 is on the 3–4 point instead of the star point. The positions are symmetrical, so it doesn't matter where Black makes a corner enclosure, at 5 or at 6. However, when White plays 6, Black must decide between an approach move at 'a' and one at 'b'.

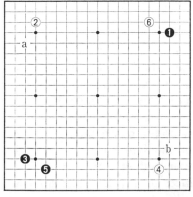

Dia. 4

Dia. 5 (Black utilizes his enclosure

Because of his corner enclosure in the lower left, Black approaches at 1. White will play a pincer somewhere on the left side, perhaps at 2, Black jumps to 3, and White extends to 4, taking some profit on the upper side. Black then plays 5. This move is both a pincer against the white stone at 2 and an ideal extension from the corner enclosure in the lower left. In the opening, you should always try to make moves which have two purposes, such as Black 5.

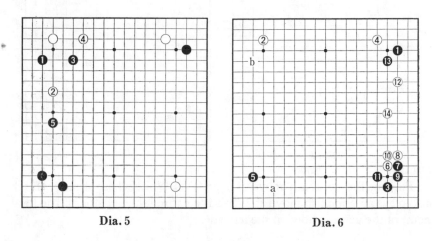

Dia. 5   Dia. 6

Dia. 6 (Corner enclosure or approach move?)

The sequence in this diagram is a variation of the famous Shusaku opening. After White secures the right side with 14, the scene of battle shifts to the left side of the board. Black must choose between making an enclosure at 'a' and approaching at 'b'.

Dia. 7 (Both a pincer and an extension)

Black should approach at 1. Making an enclosure at 2 or 'a' is not necessarily a bad move, but it is slow and unimaginative, since White will make also make an enclosure at 1; this makes the game too simple, allowing White to equalize. However, when Black approaches at 1, White must also approach at 2 to maintain the balance. Now Black 3 becomes a very effective move: it is both a pincer against White 2 and an extension from the marked stone on the right. Some readers might think that Black 3 at 'b' would make a better, tighter extension. This may be true, but then it would not be a pincer against the white stone at 2 and would only have one purpose, expanding territory.

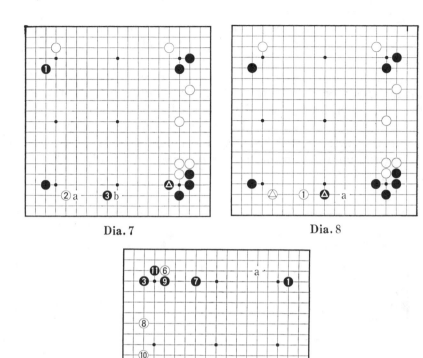

Dia. 7

Dia. 8

Dia. 9

Dia. 8 (White makes a base)

The marked black stone is not really a pincer against marked white one, because White can make a two-space extension to 1. The purpose of a pincer is to attack an isolated stone and drive it into the center. However, in this case, the marked black stone permits and seems to invite White to make a base on the lower side with 1. Next, White can aim to invade at 'a'. Moreover, Black's stone on the 3–4 point is also open to attack.

Dia. 9 (An example game)

This game was played between Sakata Eio and Kitani Minoru. After White jumps to 14, Black must decide whether to make an enclosure at 'a' or an approach at 'b'.

Dia. 10 (A corner enclosure is best)

The best move in this position is for Black to make a large-knight enclosure at 1, aiming at 3 as a follow-up. White will next make a one-space enclosure with 2, so Black extends to 3, the key point. This move not only extends from Black's own enclosure at the top right, but also limits the range of White's powerful one-space enclosure below. With respect to the choice of enclosures here, Black made a large-knight enclosure because of his position on the top left. Since the marked black stone is high, Black 1 should be low to maintain balance. On the other hand, White made a one-space enclosure with 2 because of the presence of the marked white stone, which is low.

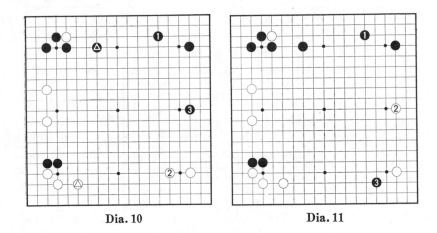

Dia. 10   Dia. 11

Dia. 11 (Make an enclosure before extending)

Because Black 3 in *Dia. 10* is such an important point, White might consider extending there with 2 before making an enclosure in the lower right. However, Black would promptly approach at 3 and be quite satisfied, having been able to make both an enclosure and an approach move. Remember, always make an enclosure before extending. It is usually premature to extend first. Extensions made without preparation seem to have a habit of ending up on the wrong point.

How to Play Handicap Go

The next three chapters are about handicap go. In handicap games, the player who takes the handicap is not as strong as his opponent. If winning (be it by only one point) is important, then it is natural for the Black player to adopt a more defensive strategy than if he were playing an even game with a player of equal strength. In a nine-stone handicap game, a good strategy for Black is to play solidly, securing certain territory right from the beginning and making sure that his groups have as few defects as possible, even it that means losing sente, or the initiative, now and then. This may not be the most elegant way of playing, but after winning a few games, the beginner will start to gain confidence, which can be just as important to his future progress as understanding advanced strategic concepts.

As the handicap decreases, the player must start to put more emphasis on attack. However, defense is still important. Even White, who must be very aggressive in handicap games, will find it to his advantage to make sure his positions are rock solid before he launches an attack. This is an important strategic principle of go: 'Don't attack until your own positions are strong.'

The following chapters analyze nine-, six-, and four-stone handicap opening strategy. Since this book is intended for players who have little experience in the game, these strategies are presented from Black's point of view. Bear in mind also that these techniques are not restricted to any one handicap: they may be used as the circumstances of actual play warrant or as the inspiration of the player dictates.

Chapter Two
The Nine-Stone Handicap and
the Attach-and-Extend Joseki

A player who takes a nine-stone handicap plays at an enormous advantage. Handicap games staged between professional players seem to indicate that to make a nine-stone handicap game completely even, that is, with a 50–50 chance for each player, a *komi* of around 140 points must be given. Therefore, if Black adopts a predominant defensive strategy he should have no difficulty in winning. In this respect, the choice of joseki is of great importance: Black will want to select a joseki which will bring sizable territory while having few weaknesses for White to exploit. The attach-and extend joseki (it begins with the attachment of Black 2 and the extension of Black 4 in *Dia. 3* on the next page) is just the one which satisfies these requirements. By playing this joseki in an 8- or 9-stone handicap game, Black can fix the style of the development around the handicap stone without causing any complications. This is ensured by the fact that White has almost no choice but to respond to Black 2 (in *Dia. 3*). Moreover, not only does Black usually secure the corner, he also develops a very powerful high position. In this chapter we will study this joseki from the standpoint of a nine-stone handicap, giving the main variations and indicating how Black should utilize his other handicap stones to attack White after the joseki is over.

Dia. 1 (Approach moves against the handicap stone)
The small-knight approach of White 1 is the most usual way for White to begin play in a handicap game. The two-space high approach at 'a' is also often seen. Other approach moves by White can be made at the points of 'b' (the one-space high approach) and 'c' (the large-knight approach). Occasionally White may even play at 'd' (Black would answer at 1), but this is really too far away to be classified as an approach move. The small-knight approach is probably the most efficient approach move, as it aims at making a corner invasion at 'e' as well as establishing a base on the side. In contrast, the approach at 'a' doesn't put much pressure on the corner and is concerned more with the center and the side.

In this book we will discuss mainly the small-knight approach of White 1. The other approach moves will be only briefly considered.

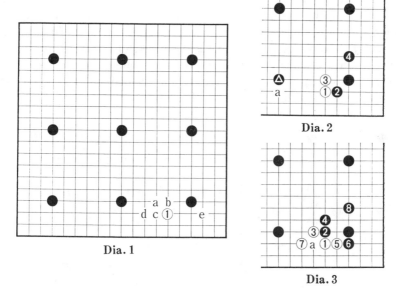

Dia. 1

Dia. 2

Dia. 3

Dia. 2 (The diagonal attachment)

One of the simplest ways for Black to answer the approach of White 1 is with the diagonal attachment of 2. White is almost forced to extend to 3, so Black maps out territory on the side with 4. The marked black stone is now very efficient, making White 1 and 3 heavy. Ideally, White would like to extend to 'a' or to where the marked black stone is, but Black is already there, so it is impossible. Eventually White will have to find a way of taking care of these two stones, but no matter what he does, he will be at a disadvantage.

Dia. 3 (The attach-and-extend joseki)

The sequence up to Black 8 shows the main variation of the attach-and extend joseki in a nine-stone game.

When Black attaches at 2, White hanes with 3, and Black extends to 4, aiming at the cut of 'a'. In order to defend against this cut, White plays 5. That gives Black a chance to secure the corner with 6. Next, White must play 7 to stave off an attack on his group. Black finally secures the area on the right side with 8. Both the black and white positions are safe, but Black conservatively has fifteen points of territory against only five for White. In addition, Black's stones are almost invulnerable to attack, but White's stones are in a precarious position. Before we consider this point, let's first see why White 7 and Black 8 were necessary.

Dia. 4 (Black plays 8 elsewhere)

If Black intends to play safely, he should not omit 8 in *Dia. 3*. If he does, White has the option of playing a second approach at 1. The sequence continues to Black 8, after which White will defend at either 'a' or 'b'; he might even play somewhere else. In a nine-stone game, White must develop quickly, so usually he will not play this sequence immediately but keep it in reserve. In any event, this possibility is a source of concern for Black, so it is better for him to defend at 8 in *Dia. 3*.

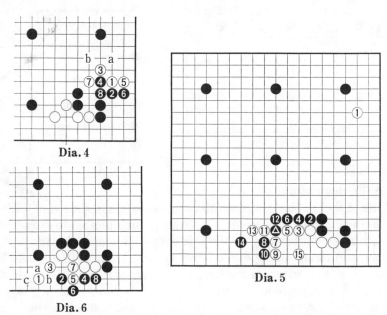

Dia. 4

Dia. 6

Dia. 5

Dia. 5 (White plays 7 elsewhere)

For his part, White must not omit 7 in *Dia. 3*. For example, if White approaches at 1, Black will press from above with 2, 4, and 6. These are now particularly effective moves, because the marked black stone is on the vital point. When White plays 7, Black continues to apply pressure from the outside with 8. The sequence to Black 14 follows; White must now play 15 to ensure life for his stones. The result is that Black has a potentially large area on the right side, influence throughout the whole board, some area in the lower left corner, and sente. He can use this sente to attack the two white stones with 'a'. For his part, White has just barely managed to live and has a profit of less than ten points. Another point to notice is that the white stones are confined to the side and have almost no strategic influence.

Dia. 6 (A variation)

Sometimes, instead of 5 in *Dia. 5*, White will jump to 1 in this diagram, hoping to confuse Black. Black should jump in at 2; after the moves to Black 8, White's stone are in serious trouble. If White does nothing, Black plays 'a', White 'b', Black 'c', and White's stones are dead. Also, note that Black 2 has occupied the same vital point as White 15 did in *Dia. 5*.

The exchange of White 7 for Black 8 in *Dia. 3* was necessary, since White will be able to take the initiative in some other part of the board regardless, he should not omit this exchange. However, Black still might get a chance to attack the four white stones after the joseki in Dia. 3. The next few diagrams show a simple and safe way of doing this.

Dia. 7 (An iron pillar)

Black 1 is like an iron pillar: strong, safe, and solid. For this reason, it is the ideal move in a nine-stone handicap game. Not only does it strengthen Black's lower left side, it also severely attacks the four white stones on the right. White is forced to run away into the center with 2. Black continues to press White with 3, building up massive thickness on the left side.

Dia. 8 (White dies)

If White ignores Black 1 and plays elsewhere, White's stones die in the sequence up to 13. There are many variations, but after 3, Black just has to remember that both the points 4 and 5 are vital to the life of the white group, so if White takes one of them, Black should take the other. The reader should study the position after Black 3 and convince himself that White has no way of making life.

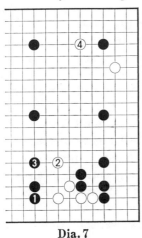

Dia. 7

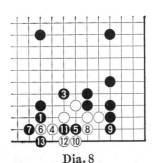

Dia. 8

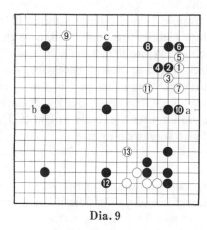

Dia. 9

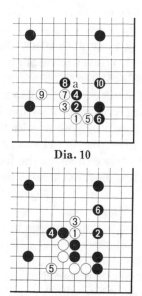

Dia. 10

Dia. 11

Dia. 9 (Proper timing)

The result in *Dia. 7* is good for Black. However, White can take the initiative there and make another approach move in the upper right corner. This could lead to complications, but Black should try to avoid a difficult game. Therefore, a reasonable strategy for Black is to play the same joseki in that corner with the sequence up to 8. At this point, White might want to slide to 'a', to reduce the territory Black has on the right side, or he might want to make another approach move at 9. If White approaches at 9, then making an iron pillar at 10 becomes a very good move. It not only solidifies the territory on the lower right side but also attacks the four white stones. After White 11, Black can also make another iron pillar with 12 at the bottom. Now after White 13, Black can answer 9. On the other hand, if White were to slide to 'a' instead of playing 9, Black should take some other big point on the board, such as 12, 'b' or 'c'. The sequence in this diagram is, admittedly, artificial, but it serves to show that the longer one waits, the stronger the iron pillar move becomes. Of course in waiting there is the risk that White may slide at 'a' first, but early in the game a move on the second line is not so big, and Black can ignore it if there is some other big strategic point to take. The conclusion to be drawn from all this is that timing is of paramount importance.

Up to this point we have studied the basic variation of the attach-and-extend joseki from the standpoint of a nine-stone handicap game. However, this variation is not the only one White can choose from; in fact, after Black 4 (in *Dia. 3*), White has many alternative ways of playing. Let's study some of these other variations.

Dia. 10 (Second variation: pushing up)

After Black blocks with 6, White could also push up with 7. If Black plays 8, White 9 is the proper response. Finally, Black must defend his defect at 'a' with 10.

Dia. 11 (The cut)

After Black hanes at 8 in *Dia. 10*, he need not fear the cut of White 1 in this diagram. Black simply responds with 2, threatening to capture White 1, so White must play 3. Next Black extends to 4, forcing White to defend with 5. Finally, Black secures the territory on the right side with 6, leaving White in a very bad situation, with his stones 1 and 3 drifting aimlessly within the sphere of Black's influence.

Dia. 12 (A future attack)

Returning to *Dia. 10*, Black might be able to attack the five white stones with 1 and 3 sometime in the future, thereby building up thickness on the left side. However, after Black 10 in Dia. 10, White might conceivably play a two-space high approach move at 'a'. Black would first play 1, forcing White 2. He would then answer 'a' with 'b'. White must now play 'c' (or else Black would play on this point, severely restricting the white stone at 'a'). Finally, Black plays 3 and the sequence continues as before. In this case, White would have two stones at 'a' and 'c' floating in the center of the board with no chance of linking up with their allies on the right.

Dia. 13 (Third variation: attaching)

After Black 4, White attaches with 5. Black answers with 6 in order to force White to defend with 9. Next Black forces with 10 and 12, and White answers with 11 and 13. The order of moves here is important and must be remembered.

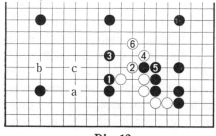

Dia. 12

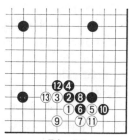

Dia. 13

Dia. 14 (The cut)

After *Dia. 13*, White can cut at 1 and take the entire corner with the moves to 5, but he ends in gote. This is too small to be played in the opening; moves like these should be reserved for the endgame.

Dia. 15 (Also too small)

Blocking at Black 1 certainly prevents the cut in *Dia. 14*, but this also ends in gote and the profit is not big enough to justify giving up sente in the opening. The maneuvers in *Dias. 14* and *15* are examples of non-urgent moves. How then should Black play following *Dia. 13*?

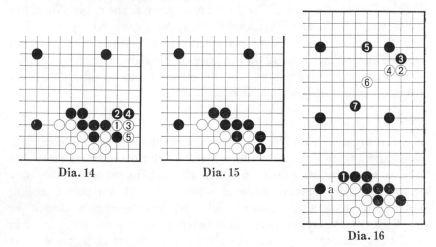

Dia. 14   Dia. 15

Dia. 16

Dia. 16 (Black utilizes all his stones)

Black 1 is a global move: Black is thinking about every stone on the board. If White attacks the upper left corner with 2, the diagonal attachment of 3 becomes a good move. The moves to 6 are a plausible continuation. Black would then continue the attack with 7, mapping out a huge area in the middle. White's stones above must fight for life. In addition, Black can severely press the white stones at the bottom with 'a' in sente.

Dia. 17 (Iron pillar)

There is a simpler way for Black to play than *Dia. 16*: the iron pillar of 1. This move emphasizes defense in contrast to the aggressive attacking style of *Dia. 16*. Black 1 is both safe and solid, as it has almost secured the entire right side. Some people would object to this move on the grounds that it doesn't make use of the marked black stone, but considering the huge advantage Black has with his handicap of nine stones, he can well afford this passive move, being compensated for it with profit and safety.

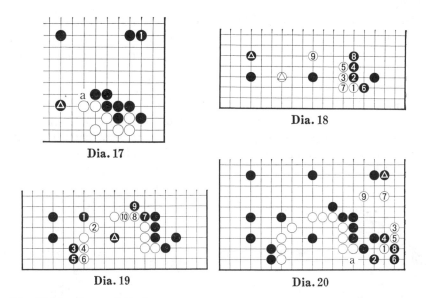

Dia. 17

Dia. 18

Dia. 19

Dia. 20

Dia. 18 (Another variation)

Assume that Black and White have exchanged the marked stones. After Black 4, White pushes up with 5, and Black takes the key point of 6, forcing White to connect at 7. Black 8 is now the proper move. Next, White caps with 9, mapping out a large area on the side. What should Black do?

Dia. 19 (Black's area is larger than White's)

Black has two alternatives. He can either run away with his marked stone or he can use the presence of this stone to expand his corner and center influence by threatening to connect to the outside as in this diagram. In a 9-stone game, this sequence is probably the best way to proceed as Black's area in the corners is much larger than the territory White has established on the side. However, after White 10 there are some things that Black must be careful about.

Dia. 20 (The 3–3 point invasion)

After the moves in *Dia. 19*, Black might make an iron pillar with the marked stone, but later White could make a 3–3 point invasion at 1. Black 2 is a good move, as it aims at 'a' while attacking White 1. The result to White 9 is good for Black, but White has taken away most of Black's territory on the right side and he now has many chances to cause complications. Consequently, this method of play cannot be recommended for a player who takes a nine-stone handicap.

Dia. 21 (The prudent way)

Black should block with 2. After the moves to Black 6, White has made some inroads into Black's corner and has expanded his area on the lower side, but at the same time Black's area on the right side has become secure.

Dia. 22 (Endgame)

After Dia. 21, there still remains a big endgame sequence. If Black can play 2 before White can play 1, he will secure the corner. On the other hand, if White can play 1 first, he will be able to prevent Black from getting the whole corner. For Black to play 2, or for White to play 1, is worth at least 8 points in gote.

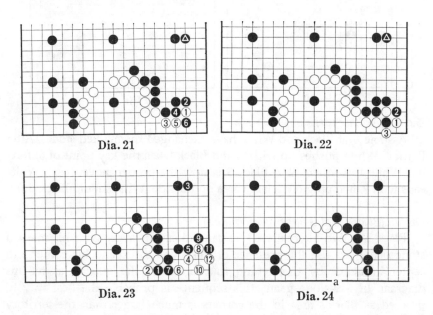

Dia. 21

Dia. 22

Dia. 23

Dia. 24

Dia. 23 (Ko)

If Black wishes to avoid the sequences shown in the last three diagrams, he can defend the corner by forcing with 1 (White will block with 2) and then make an iron pillar with 3. However, White can still invade with 4 and get a *ko* up to 12.

Dia. 24 (Descending)

Descending with Black 1 is slow, but it is the safest and steadiest move available. A move like this is especially recommended for those who want to avoid complications. Besides securing a very large corner, Black also aims at 'a' to further reduce White's area on the lower side. Having now secured a large amount of territory in two corners , Black waits to see how White will attack.

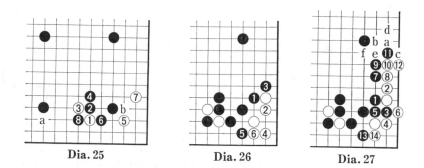

Dia. 25   Dia. 26   Dia. 27

Dia. 25 (Fourth variation: the 3–3 point invasion)

After Black extends to 4, White can immediately invade the corner at the 3–3 point with 5. The virtue of this move for White is that it can lead to many complicated variations. Theoretically, blocking at 6 is the best response, and after White 7, 8 gives Black a thick position which radiates strength throughout the whole board, while White's two stones in the corner are still vulnerable to attack. However Black must be careful, since White 1 and 3 could come to life after a white attachment at 'a'. Instead of 7, White could have played 'b'. The result would have been about the same after Black 8.

Dia. 26 (Black makes thickness)

If Black gets a chance, he can attack the White's two stones in the corner by attaching at 1. This is a very severe attack and White must draw back with 2. The sequence continues up to White 6, with Black making a tremendous outer wall, while White has made life on a very small scale in the corner. After this, Black should play elsewhere.

Dia. 27 (Extending)

White could also answer Black 1 by extending to 2. The sequence to White 14 results, and this is even better for Black than *Dia. 26*, as his thickness is even bigger. Again, Black should play in another part of the board; if White clamps at 'a', Black will play the sequence from 'b' to 'f', and his thickness will be even greater.

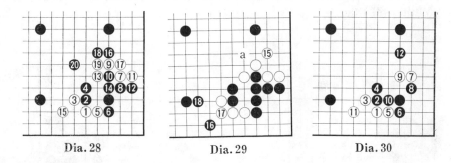

Dia. 28   Dia. 29   Dia. 30

Dia. 28 (Invading the right side)

After the moves to Black 6, there is one more variation you should know: the invasion on the right side with White 7. Diagonally attaching with 8 is the best response. With the sequence to 14, Black secures his corner and White defends his group at the bottom with 15. However, White seems to have overextended himself. Black launches an attack on the white stones on the right by clamping with 16, and after Black 20, the white stones on the right side are in bad trouble.

Dia. 29 (White defends on the other side)

If White defends the stones on the right with 15, Black launches an attack on the stones at the bottom with 16 and 18. Again White is in trouble. As an alternative to 15, White could have played at 'a', but this move would not have much effect on the endangered stones at the bottom.

Dia. 30 (Extending)

Against Black 8, if White extends to 9, Black will immediately play 10, forcing White to defend his stones at the bottom with 11. Next Black attacks White's two stones on the right with 12, and again White is in trouble. From these diagrams the conclusion is that invading the right side with White 7 in *Dia. 28* is a bit of an overplay, as his efforts are spread too thinly. White should play solidly with 7 in *Dia. 3*, and wait for a black misstep. This is a good example of why even White, who has to be aggressive in handicap games, must play defensive moves from time to time. Remember the principle: 'Don't attack until your own positions are strong.'

Chapter Three
Six-Stone Handicap Opening Strategy

In the last chapter we studied the attach-and-extend joseki in relation to a nine-stone handicap. Our analysis was restricted to one corner, but here we will consider maneuvers involving at least half the board. The positions in this chapter typically arise in 6-, 7-, 8-, and 9-stone handicap openings, and the techniques learned here can be applied in handicaps of any size.

a) White's Capping Strategy

Dia. 1 (The Cap)
White 1 is another approach move often seen in handicap games. Black's best response is to jump to 2. This high approach doesn't attack the corner as strongly as the small-knight approach; instead, it places emphasis on the side and center of the board. Against the approach of White 3, the one-space jump of Black 4 is also a good response, and is the preferred move in low-handicap games. Next, the cap of White 5 can be an effective strategy for White in high-handicap games. The virtue of this move is that it can cause complicated fighting which could spread throughout the board. Moreover, it can deliver a psychological blow to Black. Actually, however, Black has nothing to fear, as there are effective ways of dealing with this cap. We will study two black counter-strategies.

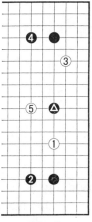

Dia. 1

Dia. 2 (Avoiding complications)

After White caps with 5, Black can sacrifice his marked stone and give White the area on the right side of the board. While doing this he will use the presence of the marked stone to expand his influence in the center with 6, 8, and 10. Note that these moves threaten to link up with the marked stone, so if White insists on carrying through with this strategy he must defend with 7, 9, and 11. Next, Black expands his corners with 12, 14, 16, and 18. White is now committed to defending this territory, so he must play 13, 15, 17 and 19. Next, Black takes a big point on the side with 20. Black's marked stone can still escape into the center with 'a', so White should play 21 if he wants to secure his territory on the side. This gives Black the opportunity to take another big point at 22. Note that Black 20 should be played before running away at 'a' in order to stabilize the upper side. (If this were a nine-stone handicap game, Black would already have a stone at 'b', so it might be all right to play 'a' immediately.) White has about 20 points of territory on the side, but Black has at least 20 points in each of his two corners as well as endgame points at 'c' and 'd'.

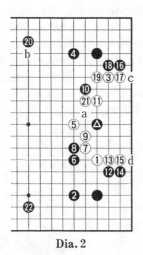

Dia. 2

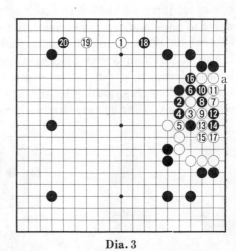

Dia. 3

Dia. 3 (White omits 19)

You might wonder why White 19 in *Dia. 2* is necessary. Wouldn't it be bigger to play this move at 1 in this diagram? The moves to White 17 should convince you otherwise. Black can later play 'a' in sente, forcing

White to capture the black stones at 12 and 14. Next, Black makes his upper corner absolutely safe by extending to 18, leading to the natural exchange of 19 and 20. In conclusion, White's territory on the right is now worth only about 12 points. Black for his part has closed off three corners (the upper left corner is worth at least 25 points in almost certain profit.

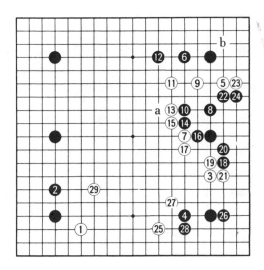

Dia. 4 (Black must not try to live on the side)

The worst thing Black can do is to try to live on the side. White does not have to kill Black. All he need do is to force him to struggle for eyes. In the meantime, White will be building up influence in the center and encroaching on Black's corners at the top and bottom. This diagram is an example of what could happen when Black on thinks of living on a small scale.

When White caps at 7 Black extends to 8. White jumps to 9 and Black also jumps out to 10. In response to 11, suppose that Black defends at 12 (the correct move would have been 12 at 'a'). White would then block Black's access to the center with 13 and 15. Black can certainly live on the left side with the moves to 24, but White builds up a strong position towards the center and his stones at 5 and 23 open up the corner for a white invasion at 'b'.

White next makes an approach move at 25. If Black again tries to live in the corner with 26 and 28, White plays 27 and 29 and a large framework territorial materializes in the center of the board.

Dia. 5 (Black resists)

After White caps at 5, Black could also try to run away with his marked stone. This is Black's best strategy, but it sometimes leads to complications.

The moves available to Black in putting this strategy into effect are 'a' to 'e'. All risk complications, but the strongest is the shoulder hit of 'd'. It is required study for all beginning players.

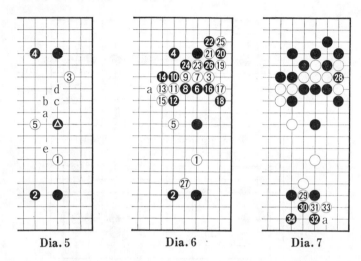

Dia. 5   Dia. 6   Dia. 7

Dia. 6 (The shoulder hit)

The shoulder hit of Black 6 is a severe response. The sequence shown here is a *joseki*. After White resists with 7 and 9, Black 10 is the crucial move. Although it looks dangerous Black has nothing to worry about, as long as he knows the follow-up. Next, White cuts at 11 and after White turns at 15 (necessary, because Black threatens to play at 'a' and capture White's two stones in a ladder), Black goes after the three white stones in the upper right with 16. A capturing race begins. White tries to make a fighting shape with 17 and 19, but Black calmly attaches with 20, another crucial move. With White 25 the position turns into a *ko*. Black captures with 26, and White makes his best *ko* threat, peeping at 27, but —

Dia. 7 (Black ignores the ko threat)

Black ignores the ko threat and captures four stones with 28, ending the ko and making a profit of at least 45 points. White pushes through with 29 to make good his *ko* threat, but after Black connects at 34, his stones on the lower side are safe. Compared to White's profit of about 15 points, Black's profit is enormous. Moreover, Black 'a' is *sente*, while if White plays here, it will be *gote*. White has gotten off to a very bad start.

Dia. 8 (A variation)

After Black *ataris* with 12 in *Dia. 5*, White could also answer with 13 as here. Black will capture with 14 and the sequence continues naturally up to Black 26, with Black securing the top as his territory. White, on the other hand, has no territory and all his stones are vulnerable to attack. In particular, Black can still attack White's stones 1 and 5 by playing 'a', White 'b', Black 'c', White 'd', Black 'e'. White will be in great trouble.

Dia. 9 (White peeps)

The peep of White 2 and the attachment of 4 are light plays. White hopes to lure Black into complications. Black 3 and 5 are calm responses which secure the corner. After White 6, Black pushes out into the center with 7, 9, and 11. This result is excellent for Black. He has solidly secured the upper right corner and the two marked white stones are weak and vulnerable in the shadow of Black's solid wall above.

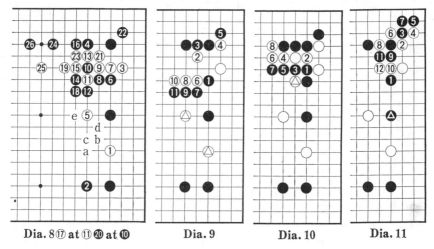

Dia. 8⑰ at ⑪ ⑳ at ❿   Dia. 9   Dia. 10   Dia. 11

Dia. 10 (Bad for Black)

When White plays the marked stone, Black must not push through with 3, 5 and 7. After White 8, the four black stones in the corner will come under severe attack.

Dia. 11 (White attaches; Black's wrong response)

White can also attach with 2. Black 3 is a natural, but for Black to answer 4 with 5 is an overplay. White will atari with 8, then push through with 10 and 12. White has turned the tables on Black. Black has failed to rescue his marked stone and the prospects for White on the right side have improved.

Dia. 12 (The correct response)

Giving *atari* from the outside with 5 is a positive way for Black to answer White 4. Up to 10, White secures the corner, while Black gets a strong position on the outside as well as profit. Black also ends with sente. Moreover, White's two marked stones are weak and loosely connected.

Dia. 13 (The high capping move)

Capping one point higher with Black 5 would seem to have the same meaning as the cap of 5 in *Dia. 5*, but there is a difference and Black should not blindly play the sequence in *Dia. 6*.

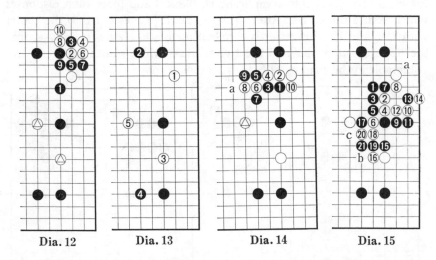

| Dia. 12 | Dia. 13 | Dia. 14 | Dia. 15 |

Dia. 14 (The ladder is bad for Black)

If Black plays the shoulder hit with 1 and continues to 9 as before, he will be in for a surprise. The ladder starting at Black 'a' no longer works because the marked white stone breaks the ladder. Consequently, White can play 10 and the position is not as simple for Black as it was.

Dia. 15 (Black succeeds)

Black 1 is one of many good responses to the high cap of 5 in *Dia. 12*. If White responds with 2, Black simply pushes with 3 and 5, after which White must cut with 6. Black next forces White to live with the moves to 13. After Black attaches with 15, he pushes through with 17, 19 and 21. White is in serious trouble: Black is threatening to play at 'a', which kills the white stones. At the same time, the two other white groups are in danger: Black is threatening to play 'b' and 'c'. There is no way White can prevent Black from making a large profit.

Dia. 16 (White fights back)

White could fight back by attaching at 2. Black answers with 3, and in the sequence to 11 Black takes the corner. White next secures his stones on the right side with the moves to 18. In the meantime, Black has built a strong position in the center with 19. With his profit in the top right corner and his outside influence, Black is in a commanding lead.

Dia. 17 (A variation)

Against Black 3, White could also extend to 4. Black secures the corner with 9, and White in turn must secure his stone on the side with 10 and 12. After 13, Black again has the lead.

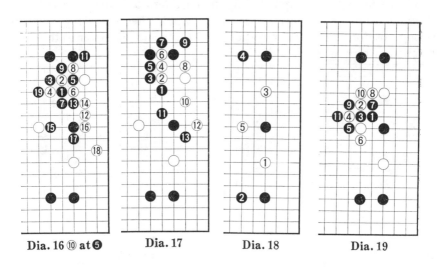

Dia. 16 ⑩ at ❺   **Dia. 17**   **Dia. 18**   **Dia. 19**

Dia. 18 (Another white strategy)

White might sometimes play two-space high-approach moves at both the top and the bottom, followed by a cap at 5. These moves place a tighter grip on the black stone in the center. The moves we have learned so far in this section are not applicable in this position. How should Black play?

Dia. 19 (Black moves out into the center)

Black should move out into the center with the diagonal move of 1. White's attempt to confine Black to the side is to no avail. With the sequence to 11, Black has easily broken out into the center and has a powerful position there. Furthermore, the two white groups above and below are now weak and vulnerable to attack. If White plays 8 at 10, Black will play at 8 himself and secure the right side.

Dia. 20 (A variation)

White could extend to 6 when Black cuts at 5. Black would then simply capture one stone with 7. Black is now in a good position. He threatens to cap at 'a' or attack White by peeping at 'b' or cutting at 'c'.

We have studied only a few of the many variations that come up in White's capping strategy. To cover all of them would require an encyclopedic volume. In summary, there are two main ways for Black to counter this strategy. The simplest way, is for Black to give up the side but to expand his corners and central influence, while reducing the scale of White's side. The other way is to resolutely run away with the capped stone into the center. This latter approach is recommended, even though it involves some risk of complicated fighting. Under no circumstances should Black try to make life on the side. White would then be able to develop strong positions towards the corners, and this could spill over to threaten Black's territory there.

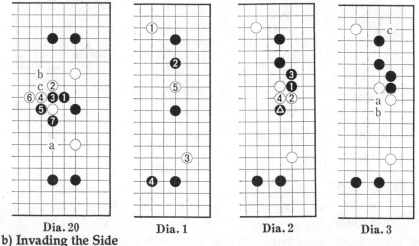

Dia. 20   Dia. 1   Dia. 2   Dia. 3

b) Invading the Side

Dia. 1 (Invasion)

In handicap games from six to nine stones, White often plays approach moves from different sides, such as 1 and 3 here. If Black responds with the one-space jumps of 2 and 4, the invasion of White 5 is a common strategy. There are many ways Black can go wrong.

Dia. 2 (A common mistake)

Answering White 5 in *Dia. 1* by attaching with 1 here is a common mistake beginners make. The sequence to 4 naturally follows, but the marked black stone has lost its value. To understand this, look at *Dia. 3*.

Dia. 3 (Why attaching is bad)

This diagram is the same a *Dia*. 2 except that White 4 and the marked black stone have been removed. Where would Black now play, 'a' or 'b'? Of course, he would cut at 'a', separating White's two stones. On the other hand, a peep at 'b', allowing White to strengthen his stones by connecting at 'a', would be a vulgar move. But this is precisely the situation in *Dia*. 2. Black might argue that he has secured his stones above and made some profit in the corner. However, this way of thinking is mistaken. To ensure this profit, Black needs another move to defend against an invasion at 'c'.

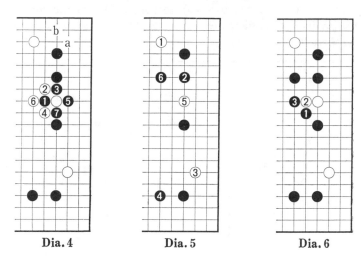

| Dia. 4 | Dia. 5 | Dia. 6 |

Dia. 4 (Attaching on top)

Attaching on top with Black 1 is also a mistake. With the moves to 6, White makes a *ponnuki* (the shape made by four stones capturing one stone) and it generates influence throughout the whole board. (There is a go proverb that says, '*Ponnuki* is worth 30 points.') Once again, Black's profit is not as large as it might appear, since White still has the possibility of invading at 'a' or sliding to 'b'. Moreover, White has *sente*.

Dia. 5 (The one-space jump)

The one space jump of Black 6 is an excellent move. It attacks both of White's stones at 1 and 5. There is a strategic principle to guide you in such situations: when you are strong and your opponent is weak, don't attach. An attaching move provokes your opponent to strengthen his stones, while your own strength will be relatively diminished. This principle is well demonstrated in this example, with the one-space jump of Black 6 being played from a position of strength.

Dia. 6 (White plays elsewhere)

The full power behind Black 6 in *Dia. 5* becomes apparent in this diagram. If White plays his next move elsewhere, Black 1 and 3 launch a severe attack on the white stones.

Dia. 7 (Two weak groups)

White might try to run away by jumping to 1. Black would then launch an attack on the stone at the bottom by attaching with 2, forcing White to extend to 3. Black 4 then strikes at the vital point of the white formation (just where White wanted to play), forcing White to run away into the center with 5. The sequence continues to 12, and White is left with two weak groups. It will be difficult to save both of them.

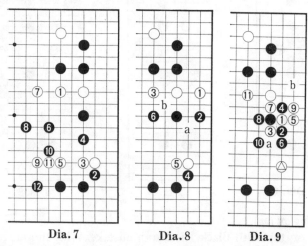

Dia. 7   Dia. 8   Dia. 9

Dia. 8 (Jumping towards the edge)

White could also jump towards the edge with 1. This move aims at 'a', enabling him to link up his stones on the right side, so Black must also jump down to 2. Since Black now threatens to attack White by playing 'b', White must run away into the center with 3. As before, Black attaches with 4 and jumps to 6. The result is similar to *Dia. 7*.

Dia. 9 (White attaches)

White could also attach at 1 after Black jumps to 6 in *Dia. 5*. Black should block with 2; the moves to White 11 follow naturally. The marked white stone is isolated within a strong black position. Moreover, White must run away with 11, since Black is threatening to destroy White's eye shape by playing at 'b'. If White had played at 'a' instead of 7, Black would have played 9 and captured two stones.

— 36 —

Dia. 10 (White makes a position at the bottom)

White could also slide to 1. Black calmly answers with 2 and White settles himself by extending to 3. The iron pillar of Black 4 is a strong move; it allows Black to link up his stones with 6, while preventing White from linking up his own stones. It also forces White to jump to 5 as Black threatens to play at 'b'. Finally, it has an effect on the three White stones below, since a black move at 'a' is a strong threat against these stones.

Dia. 11 (The diagonal attack)

Against the invasion of White's marked stone, attacking with the diagonal move of Black 1 is a forceful way of playing.

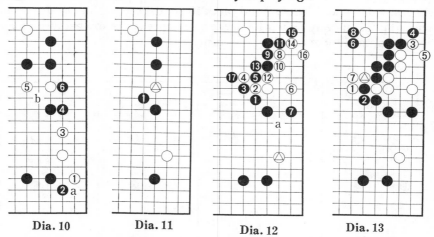

| Dia. 10 | Dia. 11 | Dia. 12 | Dia. 13 |

Dia. 12 (White makes a small profit on the side)

Against Black 1, it's hard for White to break out into the center. First White plays 2 and 4, then jumps towards the edge with 6, aiming to link up with his marked stones by playing 'a'. Black prevents this by jumping to 7. The sequence to 16 naturally follows and White has made life on the side. Finally, Black plays 17, capturing the white stone on the outside in a ladder. The result here is better for Black: his outside influence more than outweighs the small profit made by White's isolated group on the side.

Dia. 13 (A variation)

Instead of 14 in *Dia. 12*, White plays 1 here to forestall the ladder mentioned in the previous diagram. Black connects at 2, and White lives with 3 and 5. Next, Black plays the shoulder hit of 6, threatening to capture the marked white stone. When White connects with 7, Black plays 8, gaining a large profit in the corner.

Dia. 14 (Extending)

Against Black 3, White might extend to 4. In this case, attaching at 5 is the best move. White must answer with 6, since Black 5 threatens to capture the three white stones below. Next, Black secures the corner with 7. The moves to Black 13 follow. White's result is a catastrophe; his stones in the center have no eyes and are vulnerable to attack, while Black has almost secured the top right corner.

Dia. 15 (Establishing a position on the upper side)

If White wanted to establish a position on the upper side, he would first play 1, then turn at 3. After Black cuts with 4, White plays two forcing moves with 5 and 7. White 9 and Black 10 are the same as in *Dia. 14*. White should play this way only if he needs a presence at the top because he has lost the possibility of invading the corner.

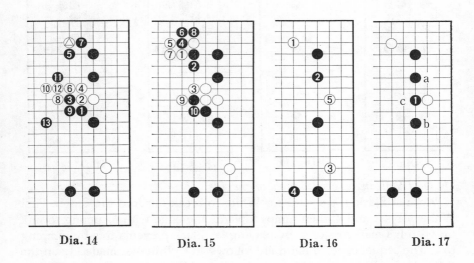

Dia. 14   Dia. 15   Dia. 16   Dia. 17

Dia. 16 (A deep invasion)

In this variation, White makes a deep invasion into Black's sphere of influence with 5. Black must take a different approach in responding to this move.

Dia. 17 (Attaching)

Attaching with Black 1 is the correct response. If Black were to play 'a' or 'b' instead, White would simply jump to 'c' and escape into the center.

Dia. 18 (A good result for Black)

If White wedges in with 1, Black will *atari* with 2 and block with 4. White has little choice but to play the sequence through to 13, after which Black jumps to 14, making a magnificent wall on the outside. On the other hand, White has been forced to crawl submissively along the third line.

Dia. 19 (A powerful pincer)

Instead 5 in *Dia. 18*, White can attach at 1. Black wedges in with 2, and after White 7, Black plays 8 in *sente*. Next Black attaches with 10, making the corner invasion-proof (because of the presence of 8). After White 11, Black attacks these stones with 12, a powerful pincer because of Black's strong wall on the right.

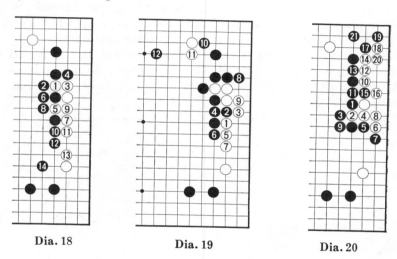

Dia. 18   Dia. 19   Dia. 20

Dia. 20 (A variation)

Against Black 1, White can also wedge in at 2 on the other side. Up to 20, White makes a living group on the side while Black has a massive wall that radiates influence throughout the whole board. Considering this result, White 1 in *Dia. 18* is preferable for White since there are more possibilities for complications.

Chapter Four

Four-Stone Handicap and the One-Space Jump Joseki

In this chapter, we will thoroughly study the one-space jump response to the small-knight approach against a star point stone. The *josekis* that result from these white and black moves are very important in modern go, being used in even games as well as handicap games. A star point stone emphasizes the center, so to answer an approach against this stone with a move on the fourth line is consistent with the strategic aims of playing on the star point in the first place. This does not mean that a small-knight or a large-knight extension from a star point stone is bad. Depending on the position, such moves are sometimes better. However, in order to become a well-rounded player with a good attacking style, it is necessary that you learn these *josekis*.

Dia. 1

Dia. 2

A Survey of the One-Space Jump Joseki

Dia. 1 (The one-space jump)

Against the small-knight approach of White 1, the one-space jump of Black 2 is a strong and aggressive move. It is recommended for use in handicap games of five stones or less. This move emphasizes attack and quick development towards the center and side. It is weak defensively, since White can attack at 'a', aiming at several weak points in the corner. However, Black can successfully meet any attack that White might launch.

Dia. 2 (The small-knight response)

Against White 1, Black could also have extended to 2 or 'a'. These moves are more defensive than Black 2 in *Dia. 1*, but in some positions they could be the best moves.

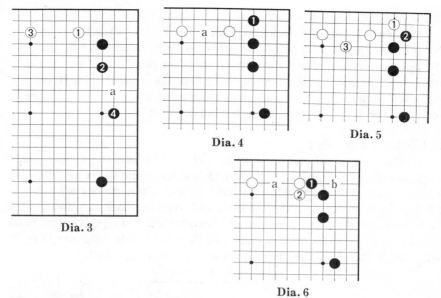

Dia. 3

Dia. 4

Dia. 5

Dia. 6

Dia. 3 (Three-space extension)

One continuation after Black 2 is for White to make a three-space extension to 3. Next, Black takes the big point at 4. His position on the right side is now stable because the weak point at 'a' has been defended.

Dia. 4 (No hurry)

Black hopes to be able to take the territory in the corner by jumping to 1. This move also aims at invading at 'a'. However, proper timing is important; Black should be in no hurry to take this point. If White invades at the 3–3 point first, Black should confine him to the corner and get his compensation from outside influence.

Dia. 5 (Sliding into the corner)

White could also slide into the corner with 1. Black defends with 2, and White must make shape with 3. White gets a solid position at the top, but, unfortunately for him, Black's territory on the right also becomes strong and White ends in *gote*.

Dia. 6 (The diagonal attachment)

Black must not diagonally attach with 1. This move provokes White 2, so Black's chance to invade at 'a' disappears (White's three-space extension from his stones on the right is now perfect). Moreover, White can still invade the corner with 'b'. This move will be discussed in more detail later.

Dia. 7 (When to diagonally attach)

After exchanging the marked stones, White might play somewhere else. Now the diagonal attachment of Black 1 becomes an effective move. After 2, Black pincers with 3 and the two white stones come under severe attack. Black next threatens to attack at 'c'. Note how the marked black stone supports this attack. This is why the one-space jump is the preferred response to White 1 in *Dia. 1*, as opposed to the moves 'a' or 'b'.

Dia. 8 (White's invasion)

If White wants the corner he invades at 1. The moves to 9 follow. Pushing through and cutting with 11 and 13 enables White to create defects in Black's shape. Finally, White lives with 15, and Black catches the stone at 13 in a ladder with 16. If the ladder is unfavorable, Black can also play at 'a' to capture this stone. (Confirm this for yourself. Note the marked black stone.) White has taken the corner, but Black's outside influence is overwhelming. Therefore, the timing of this invasion is important.

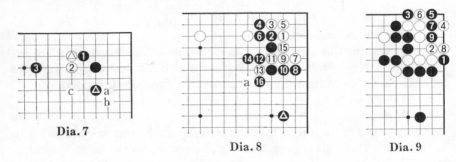

Dia. 7   Dia. 8   Dia. 9

Dia. 9 (White dies)

White cannot omit playing 15 in *Dia. 8*. Black can kill White's stones in the corner with 1 and 3, followed by the moves to 9.

Dia. 10 (Ko)

If White plays elsewhere after 10 in *Dia. 8*, Black can start a *ko* for the life of the white stones in the corner, beginning with 1 and 3. The *ko* starts with Black 7 and 9. This *ko* fight would usually be bad for White, but if he has a lot of *ko* threats, it might be possible for him to play this way.

Dia. 11 (The order of moves)

In order for Black to set up the *ko*, the order of moves in *Dia. 10* is important. If Black pushes in with 3 before playing 5, White can get two eyes with the sequence to 14.

Dia. 12 (Black is short of liberties)

After White captures four stones with 14 in *Dia. 11*, Black can't start a *ko* with 15. After White 18, Black can't connect at 16 because he has no liberties, so when White takes these two stones, he gets two eyes.

Dia. 13 (White dies unconditionally)

If White captures with 4 after 3, Black will kill the white stones with 5 and 7. White 8 is to no avail as Black 9 and the marked stone keep White confined. Study *Dias. 8 to 13*, since this invasion occurs frequently .

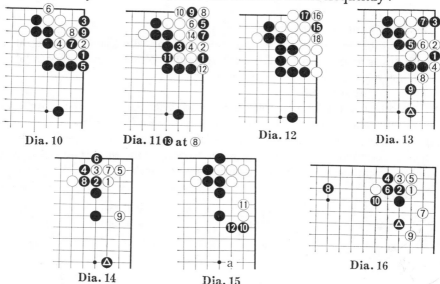

Dia. 10   Dia. 11 ⑬ at ⑧   Dia. 12   Dia. 13

Dia. 14   Dia. 15   Dia. 16

Dia. 14 (A variation)

White 5 is another variation of this invasion. Black first *ataris* with 6, then connects with 8. White can now extend to 9. Black should be satisfied with his outside influence and play his next move somewhere else.

Dia. 15 (Attaching)

If the marked stone in *Dia. 14* is not present, Black should attach at 10, then draw back to 12. If Black had a stone at 'a', however, it would be so close to 10 and 12 that it would be redundant.

Dia. 16 (Black takes the top)

If White invades at 1 in answer to the marked stone, Black should extend to 8 after White 7. If White next plays 9, Black makes good shape with 10. Depending on the circumstances, the order of 8 and 10 can be reversed.

Dia. 17 (Black ends with sente)

Against White's invasion with 1, Black can take the territory on the right side by blocking at 4 after the exchange of 2 and 3. Black takes *sente* with 6.

Dia. 18 (White's stones are safe)

If Black uses his *sente* to attack White with 1, White must play 2. After 4, White's stones in the corner are absolutely safe. Later, 'a' will be a big endgame point for White.

Dia. 19 (If White doesn't respond)

If White doesn't reply to the marked stone, Black will connect at 1. White lives with 2 and 4, but Black can confine White to the top with 'a'.

Dia. 20 (White attaches)

Another way White can play is to attach with 3. After exchanging 5 for 6, White makes shape with 7. The moves to 8 are a *joseki*. Black 6, however, is a bit slow, since it allows White to play 7 and get good shape for making eyes. Nevertheless, Black has been able to occupy the important point of 8, so this would be a good result in a four-stone handicap game.

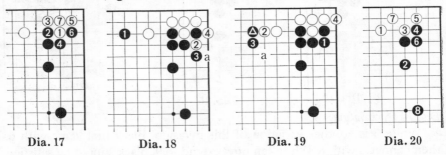

Dia. 17   Dia. 18   Dia. 19   Dia. 20

Dia. 21 (A severe move)

Black 4 here is more severe. Next, White must connect at 5. After 6, Black's shape on the right side is ideal. On the other hand, White's stones lack the eye-making potential of *Dia. 20*.

Dia. 22 (Ko)

If White answers 4 with 5, Black *ataris* with 6. If White connects at 'a' he is left with bad shape, so he might want to start a *ko* by playing at 'b'. In the opening, however, there are no *ko* threats big enough to force Black to answer, so Black will win the *ko*. Therefore, these moves are not recommended. If White does start a *ko*, he should first exchange 'c' for 'd'.

Dia. 23 (Joseki)

In answer to White 1, Black 2 is the standard move. The sequence to Black 10 follows and is a *joseki*. Now 'a' is an important point for both.

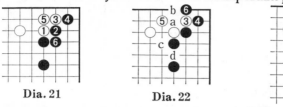

Dia. 21   **Dia. 22**

Dia. 23

Dia. 24 (Another joseki)

Sliding to 3 and extending tightly to 5 is another *joseki*. At this point it would be natural for Black to stabilize the right side by extending to 6. Locally, the vital point now for both sides will be 'a'.

Dia. 25 (White attacks)

If Black omits 6 in *Dia. 24*, White might attack at 1. Black 2 is now essential to make a base and ensure the life of his stones.

Dia. 26 (Black is eyeless)

Look what happens if Black neglects to play 2 in *Dia. 25*. White plays 1, 3, and 5. Now Black's group has no eyes, so it is very weak.

Dia. 27 (Pincer)

When White slides to 3, Black can make central thickness with the pincer at 4. White takes the corner with 5, and up to 10 Black gets central influence. Later, White can aim at 'a'. However, Black can play 4 only if the ladder is favorable for him. (See *Dia. 29* on the next page.)

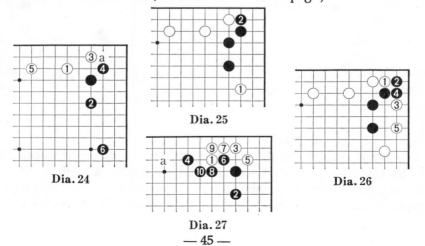

Dia. 25

Dia. 24

Dia. 26

Dia. 27

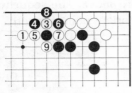

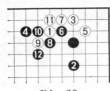

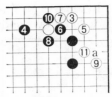

| Dia. 28 | Dia. 29 | Dia. 30 |

Dia. 28 (Linking up with a ko)

So that you understand how strong a move 'a' in *Dia. 27* is, we show what happens if Black doesn't answer White 1 here. White gets a *ko* with the moves to 9. If he wins this *ko*, he will be able to link up his group in the corner to the outside.

Dia. 29 (Threatening a ladder)

If White wanted to threaten a ladder, he could play 9 after Black 8. Black must now capture 9 in a ladder with 12. This variation would be a good strategy for Black if he wanted to make a ladder-block threat in the lower left part of the board. However, playing this sequence loses the threat of the *ko* in *Dia. 28*.

Dia. 30 (Corner profit)

If profit in the corner is most important for White, then he should play 9 after Black 8. Black plays 10, and White must play at 11 to defend against the attachment of Black 'a'.

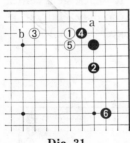

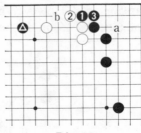

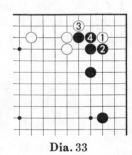

| Dia. 31 | Dia. 32 | Dia. 33 |

Dia. 31 (Overconcentrated)

If White doesn't like the pincer at 4 in *Dia. 27*, he might extend to 3 instead of sliding at 'a'. Black could attach diagonally with 4. After 5, White's shape is overconcentrated, since 3 should be at 'b', following the proverb 'extend three spaces from a two-stone wall!' Black plays 4 not so much to protect his corner, but to make White's stones overconcentrated. However, White's position becomes stronger.

Dia. 32 (3–3 point invasion)

If White invades at 1, blocking at 2 is one variation. Another answer is for Black to descend to 3. The choice depends on the circumstances. After Black 4, White can play elsewhere or continue as in the next diagram.

Dia. 33 (Continuation)

Usually White plays 5, and after Black 6 he plays elsewhere. However, there are some interesting endgame moves that you should know.

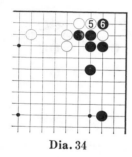

Dia. 34

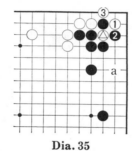

Dia. 35

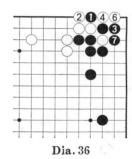

Dia. 36

Dia. 34 (Endgame moves)

In the endgame, White can reduce Black's corner by playing at 1 and 3 in *gote*. It is equally large for Black to capture at 2 before White can play these moves. (It is worth eight points in *gote*.) White should not play 1 and 3 too soon because 'a' could become a strong move, since it would threatens to save his marked stone by descending to 2.

Dia. 35 (Eliminating White's threats)

If Black doesn't like White 1 and 3 in *Dia. 34*, he can play 1 and 3 here. After White captures with 4, Black plays elsewhere with 5. However, White can play 6 in *sente* whenever he wants.

Dia. 36 (Profit in the corner)

White may not want to play 5 in *Dia. 33* because if he can later play 1 as a threat at the top (that is, affecting a fight at the top), Black may not have time to answer at 'a'. White could then play 3, taking profit in the corner.

Dia. 37 (Variation)

Instead of 4 in *Dia. 33*, Black could also play 4 as here. In the sequence to 8, White reduces Black's corner and stabilizes his stones at the top. White can now play 9 in another part of the board.

Dia. 38 (Depending on the situation)

Suppose that White's stones are surrounded as here. After Black 6, White would not play at 'b', as in *Dia. 37*, but at 7. Now when Black takes two stones with 8, White connects to the outside with 9. On the other hand, if Black plays 8 at 'a', White 9 at 8 takes the corner territory.

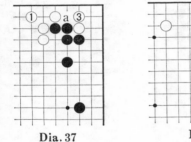

Dia. 37

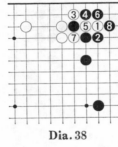

Dia. 38

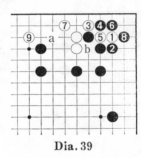

Dia. 39

Dia. 39 (Descending)

Black could also answer the invasion of White 1 by descending to 2. White lives in the corner with the moves to 13, and Black gets powerful outside influence and *sente*. White must not play 9 at 13. If he does, Black will play at 9 and White will be confined to a small life in the corner.

Dia. 40

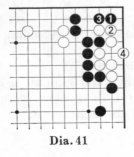

Dia. 41

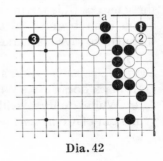

Dia. 42

Dia. 40 (Black makes profit in sente)

White 13 in *Dia. 39* is necessary. If White omitted, Black will play here with 1. After 4, White is alive, but Black has made some profit in *sente*. Black even has another way of playing.

Dia. 41 (Two threats)

After White connects at 2, Black can attack White's three stones with a pincer at 3. Black holds the move at 'a' in reserve. This move will threaten to kill White's stones in the corner and could also have an effect on White's stones at the top.

Dia. 42 (White's mistake)

Against Black 1, blocking at White 2 would be a serious mistake. After the sequence to 11, Black's five stones leave the white group with a dead shape. Having played as far as 4, White's last hope to salvage the situation would be to start a *ko* by playing 6 at 'a'.

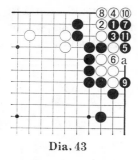

Dia. 43

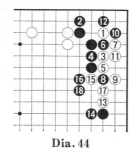

Dia. 44

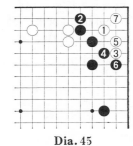

Dia. 45

Dia. 43 (Black takes the corner)

If Black wants to take the corner, he will cut at 10. Up to 18, White lives in *sente*, but Black gets both some profit in the corner and outside influence.

Dia. 44 (Passive)

It is passive for White to play the knight's move with 3. After the moves to 7, Black has *sente* and White is confined to the corner, with very little profit.

The One-Space Jump in Four-Stone Handicap Openings

In the preceding section, we studied the standard variations of the one-space jump *josekis* without considering more than one corner. In this section, we will consider this *joseki* with respect to at least half the board and particularly with respect to the four-stone handicap opening.

a) The Pincer

Dia. 1 (An ideal pincer)

After Black jumps to 2, the approach of White 3 is often played in four- and five-stone handicap games. This move strikes at the underbelly of Black's two-stone shape above. Because of the marked stone in the lower corner, the pincer of Black 4 is an ideal move: it both attacks the white stone at 3 and expands Black's position on the lower side. Running away with Black 'a' would be a passive way to play, since White could extend to 4, making a stable position on the right side. This pincer is very important in four- and five-stone openings, so we will make a thorough study of it.

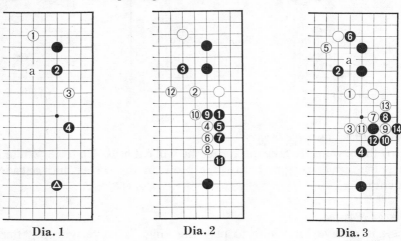

Dia. 1   Dia. 2   Dia. 3

Dia. 2 (An overplay)

The pincer of Black 1 here is an overplay. White answers by jumping to 2, and Black also jumps to 3. Next, White plays a shoulder hit at 4, forcing Black to crawl along the third line. After jumping to 12, White is satisfied, since his outside thickness is superior to Black's small profit.

Dia. 3 (Joseki)

After Black pincers with 4 in *Dia. 1*, jumping out into the center with White 1 is the natural move. Black must also jump into the center with 2. White caps with 3 and Black answers with 4. White next plays 5, aiming to peep at 'a', so Black must defend with 6. White plays the moves from 7 to 13 in order to stabilize his stones on the right side. Note the cut of 9, which is played to give White the forcing moves of 11 and 13. Black must capture with 14, and White shifts his attention elsewhere. Let's study the reasons behind all these moves in more detail.

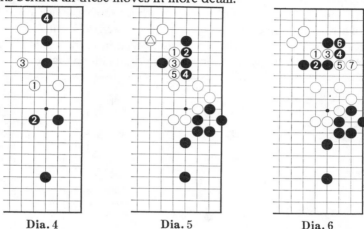

Dia. 4	Dia. 5	Dia. 6

Dia. 4 (Black is confined to the corner)

Jumping to Black 2 in answer to White 1 is passive, because White will confine Black to the corner with 3. Even after Black defends with 4, his stones are still subject to attack. That's why Black should jump to 3. As a general principle in handicap go, it is usually bad to allow White to confine your stones like this.

Dia. 5 (The peep)

If Black fails to attach at 6 in *Dia. 3* in response to the marked stone in this diagram, the peep of White 1 becomes a powerful attack. Up to 5 White makes massive thickness towards the center, while Black's stones in the corner are in danger.

Dia. 6 (Black's group is drifting aimlessly in the center)

In answer to White 1, Black could connect at 2. White will push through and cut with 3 and 5. After 7, Black has three stones drifting aimlessly in the center. Moreover, the three black stones in the corner are still not safe.

Dia. 7 (White fails)

Once Black has played the marked stone (6 in *Dia. 3*), White's tactics fail. Suppose White first makes two forcing moves with 1 and 3, then peeps with 5. After White 11, Black's corner is absolutely safe, so Black launches his own attack with 12 and 14. White's stones at the top are in serious trouble.

Dia. 8 (An effective move)

White plays the sequence from 7 to 13 in *Dia. 3* in order to give his stones a fighting shape. If White neglects these moves, Black can play 1. This looks like a strange move, but it's very effective. White's stones are now floating in the center without a base. Black next threatens 'a', White 'b', Black 'c', leaving the white stones on the right side in disarray.

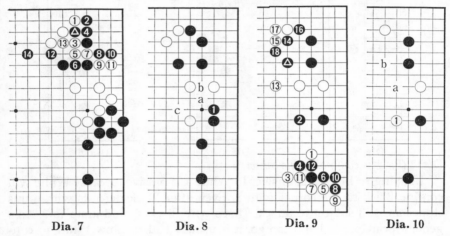

Dia. 7   Dia. 8   Dia. 9   Dia. 10

Dia. 9 (A variation)

After Black plays the marked stone (Black 2 in *Dia. 3*), the approach of White 1 here is another variation. Jumping to 2 is a good response, even though it lets White make another approach move at 3. Black now moves out into the center with 4. This allows White to take the corner with the moves to 11, but Black gets a substantial amount of territory on the right after he connects with 12. White next escapes into the center with 13, and Black strengthens his stones at the top with 14, 16 and 18. This result is good for Black, since White's three stones in the center can be attacked.

Dia. 10 (A premature cap)

Sometimes White will cap at 1 without exchanging 'a' for 'b'. This is not a good move, but White will occasionally play like this to confuse Black.

Dia. 11 (Passive)

Black 2 may seem to be the natural response to 1, but since the exchange of 'a' for 'b' hasn't been made, it is too passive. White stabilizes his stones with the moves to 9, then threatens to confine Black to the top with 11. Black diagonally extends to 12 and White strengthens his position on the right with 13. White again threatens to confine Black to the top corner by playing at 'a', so Black must run away into the center. This result is not necessarily bad for Black, but White seems to have seized the initiative.

Dia. 12 (Aggressive)

The shoulder hit of Black 2 is an aggressive move, since it immediately separates the white stones. This move is a strong response to the cap of White 1, the situation could become complicated. White 3 is a light answer; and the moves to Black 14 are natural. Black's result is very good, as he has both profit and thickness.

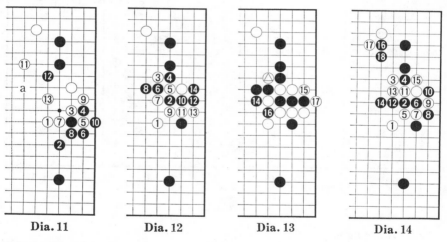

Dia. 11　　　Dia. 12　　　Dia. 13　　　Dia. 14

Dia. 13 (Greedy)

Black must not become too greedy and *atari* at 14, because White would play 15 and 17, rescuing his stones above. This would be bad for Black, as he doesn't get the profit he made in *Dia. 12*. Moreover, the marked stone is separating Black into two groups.

Dia. 14 (White comes under attack)

Instead of 5 in *Dia. 12*, White could also extend diagonally with 5. The sequence up to White 15 results, but Black attaches and extends with 16 and 18. Suddenly, the group of five white stones below comes under a severe attack.

Dia. 15 (Black makes a large profit)

Instead of 15 in *Dia. 14*, White could play 15 here. Black would answer with 16, making a large profit on the right.

Dia. 16 (A bad result for Black)

Against White 5, Black must not block at 6, because White can confine him to the corner with the sequence to 10. Black must now look after his stones there, and whatever profit he makes will be small. Compared to *Dia. 14* or *16*, this result is very bad for Black.

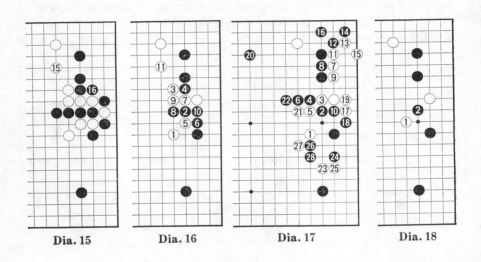

| Dia. 15 | Dia. 16 | Dia. 17 | Dia. 18 |

Dia. 17 (Pushing up)

Pushing up with White 3 against Black 2 is another variation. Black blocks this advance with 4 and White cuts with 5. The key move in this variation is Black 6. White must now make life at the top right with the moves to 19, after which Black takes a big point at the top with 20. White's maneuvers up to 27 are useless; he is left with two weak groups under attack.

Dia. 18 (The diagonal jump)

White can also play the diagonal jump of 1. Black should strike between the two stones at 2 in order to separate them. This is Black's best counter.

Dia. 19 (Joseki)

After Black 2, White jumps out to 3 and then both players connect to the center with 4 and 5. The sequence to White 19 is a *joseki*. This is a good result for Black. He has taken profit at the top and his stones there are secure. Moreover, he has made a strong position below and has *sente*.

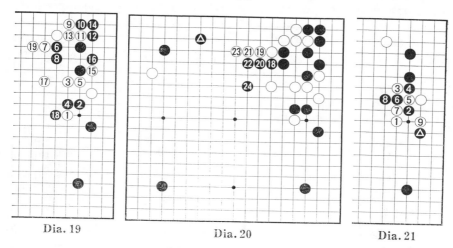

Dia. 19   Dia. 20   Dia. 21

Dia. 20 (Depending on circumstances)

If the marked black stone were present, Black could push White along the fourth line with 18, 20 and 22 instead of playing 18 in Dia. 19. He would then follow up by jumping to 24, attacking the white stones on the right. This sequence should only be played if Black has a strong position at the top left. Otherwise, the profit White gains by running along the 4th line with 19, 21 and 23 would be too big.

Dia. 21 (Bad for Black)

Against White 3, Black must not push through and cut with 4 and 6. After the *atari* of 7 White makes good shape with 9 while nullifying the effect of the marked black stone. Moreover, White's stone at 3 is splitting Black into two groups, so Black must make another move to capture it.

Dia. 22 (A simple way for Black)

The simplest way for Black to handle this variation is to descend to 6 when White plays 5. After White 7, Black secures the corner with 8. However, Black is confined to the corner and White has *sente*, so this result is inferior to *Dia. 19*. In certain circumstances, however, it may be good enough.

Dia. 23 (Pushing out into the center)

White can also push out into the center with 5 and 7 and then confine Black to the corner with 9. However, Black can easily secure life for his stones with the sequence to 14. The result here is good for Black, as his thickness is very effective. White 1 has become a useless stone. Further, Black 8 is on the vital point to nullify White's thickness on the upper side.

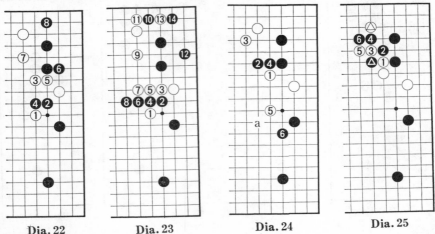

Dia. 22   Dia. 23   Dia. 24   Dia. 25

Dia. 24 (The small-knight move)

Against the knight move of 1, jumping to 2 is a good move. White plays 3, and Black defends at 4. White next plays 5, making a flexible shape. Black 6 is the key point, aiming to attack White's group at 'a'.

Dia. 25 (Pushing through and cutting)

When Black plays the marked stone, he doesn't have to worry about White pushing through and cutting with 1 and 3. Black 4 and 6 give Black a large profit at the top and the marked white stone has lost its value. At the same time, the marked black stone is still a source of worry for White.

Dia. 26 (Passive)

Answering White 1 with the knight move of 2 is passive. It doesn't put pressure on White's stones below 1, so White can take the time to stabilize his stones at the top with 3 and 5. Black's stones in the corner lack power.

Dia. 27 (Bad for Black)

Pushing through and cutting with 2 and 4 is also bad. White extends to 5, making Black 6 necessary. After exchanging 7 for 8, White takes the key point of 9. Black's result is bad, since 4 and 6 are drifting in the center.

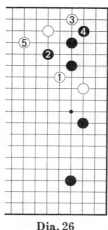

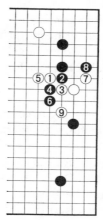

Dia. 26   Dia. 27

Dia. 28 (Peeping underneath)

After Black plays the marked stone, White also has the option of peeping at 1. Black connects with 2, and White makes a position on the right with 3. Black 4 secures a base in the corner. Next Black will aim at 'a', in order to attack the marked white stone at the top.

Dia. 29 (Variation)

After White plays the marked stone, turning with Black 1 and playing *atari* at 3 are severe moves. Black blocks at 5, and White stabilizes his stones at the top with 6, 8. and 10. Black 11 is now a powerful move. If White plays at 'a' instead of 10 to make shape on the right, Black will attack the three white stones at the top by playing at 10 himself.

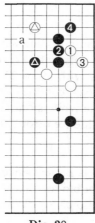

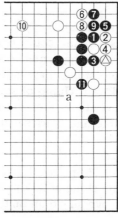

Dia. 28   Dia. 29

Dia. 30 (Premature)

After White 3 in *Dia. 28*, it would be premature for Black to attack with 1. White responds by taking profit in the corner with 2 and 4, ending in *sente*. Black's profit is not large, since the marked stone can cause trouble. Black needs another move before he can consider the top secure territory.

Dia. 31 (Overplay)

White 4 and 6, trying to confine Black's stones, are overplays. However, Black must be careful, since there are many ways he can go wrong.

Dia. 32 (Pushing through and cutting)

After White 6 in *Dia. 31*, Black should push through and cut with 7 and 9. White will draw back with 10, whereupon attaching with Black 11 is the key move. The moves to 15 naturally follow. This is a good result for Black.

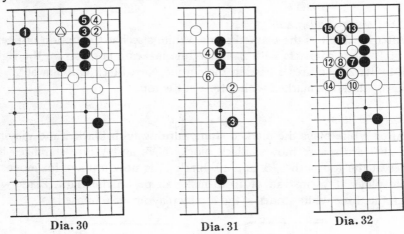

Dia. 30   Dia. 31   Dia. 32

Dia. 33 (White resists)

Against 11, White could resist with 12 and 14, but with 15 Black has gained access to the center. After 16, Black cuts with 17, then, instead of capturing two stones in a ladder, squeezes with 19 to 23, leaving White with an awkward clump of stones. Next, Black confines White to the top with the moves to 38, then extends to 39. The white stones on the right are now in trouble, and Black's wall radiates influence throughout the board.

Dia. 34 (Variation)

Instead of 26 in *Dia. 33*, White 26 here is better, since White ends in *sente*, and the stone at 26 can still cause trouble for Black. However, considering the overall situation, this result is also bad for White.

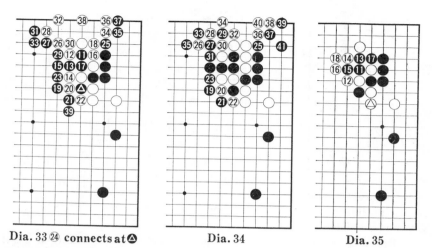

Dia. 33 ㉔ connects at ▲   Dia. 34   Dia. 35

Dia. 35 (White confines Black to the corner)

After White plays the marked stone, it is bad for Black to play 11. White simply sacrifices a stone, and Black finds himself confined to the corner.

Dia. 36 (Also bad for Black)

The sequence to 26 is also possible, but again this is bad for Black. Black's territory in the corner is not really so big, since White can still invade at 'a'. Moreover, White's influence dominates the whole board.

Dia. 37 (Black makes a big profit)

Extending into the center with 10 is a mistake. Black can take territory on the right by running along the fourth line with the moves to 15.

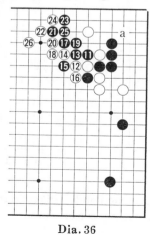

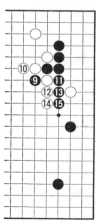

Dia. 36   Dia. 37

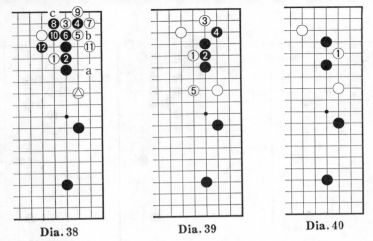

| Dia. 38 | Dia. 39 | Dia. 40 |

Dia. 38 (The slide)

After peeping at 1, White will sometimes slide to 3. Attaching at 4 is the correct way for Black to respond. After 12, White can link up with the marked stone by playing 'a'. White cannot omit 11, since Black would immediately play there himself, forcing White to play at 'b' to make two eyes. Black 'c' would then be *sente* for Black.

Dia. 39 (Passive)

Answering White 3 with the diagonal move of 4 is passive. After White jumps to 5, the moves 1 and 2 have become a good exchange for White.

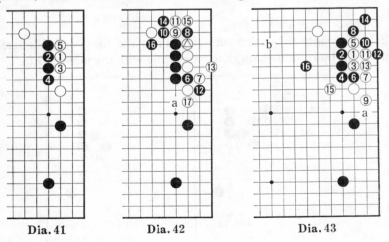

| Dia. 41 | Dia. 42 | Dia. 43 |

Dia. 40 (Peeping underneath)

Peeping underneath with White 1 immediately strikes at the weak underbelly of Black's formation. There are many continuations from here.

Dia. 41 (The vital point)

Connecting at Black 2 is the only move. White next plays 3 and Black takes the vital point of 4. What happens after White 5?

Dia. 42 (Excellent for Black)

After White plays the marked stone, Black will push through at 6, then block at 8. If White cuts with 9, Black gives White the corner and makes a wall on the outside. Note Black 12: it forces White to answer with 13. Even after White plays 17, Black can confine White to the side by playing at 'a'. Because of his outside thickness, this result is excellent for Black.

Dia. 43 (Black takes the corner)

If White answers 8 by connecting at 9, Black will take the corner with the sequence to 14. After 16, Black can play at either 'a' or 'b', depending on how White plays.

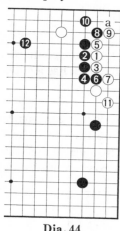

Dia. 44

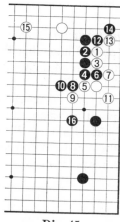

Dia. 45

Dia. 44 (Another variation)

White 9 is another variation. Black 10 is the proper response and White 11 cannot be omitted. Black 12 is the natural move, extending from the wall on the right. The point 'a' will be a big endgame move.

Dia. 45 (Pushing out into the center)

White could also push out into the center with 5. After 6, Black blocks White's advance with 8. When White connects with 11, Black takes the vital point of 12. The exchange of 13 for 14 prevents Black from taking this point with *sente*. Finally White stabilizes his position at the top with 15 and Black jumps to 16. This is a good result for Black.

Dia. 46 (An even result)

After White blocks with 7, Black can also cut at 8. The result to Black 16 is even: White has profit and Black has a thick position facing the center. However, Black started with an advantage, so he should expect a better result than this.

Dia. 47 (Cutting on the wrong side)

Black mustn't cut with 8 on this side. After Black takes two stones with 12, White slides to 13 and Black's stones have become overconcentrated while White has established bases at the top and on the right side.

Dia. 48 (Good for Black)

After White 3, Black 4 is also possible. White takes the other vital point at 5. Black 6 is a forcing move which makes it hard for White to make two eyes. After exchanging 8 for 9, Black jumps to 10, and Black can attack one of the two white groups. This result is good for Black.

Dia. 49 (Connecting with the knight move)

If White plays 3 immediately, Black turns at 4. Black connects at 8, and White links up with a knight move at 9. After 10, Black has a good result.

Dia. 50 (The 3–3 point invasion)

The 3–3 point invasion at 1 is another way White can answer Black's pincer (the marked stone). Black should give up the corner and take up position at the top with the moves to 10. Considering that Black has a stone on the star point in the top left, this is an excellent result for him.

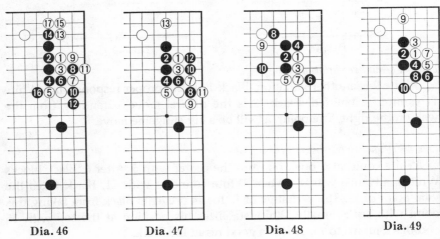

Dia. 46   Dia. 47   Dia. 48   Dia. 49

Black must not attack the white stones in the corner with 8. If he does, he will fail because of the presence of the marked white stone. White captures three black stones with 15.

Dia. 52 (Also bad)

The moves in this diagram were given as a *joseki* in *Dia. 17* on page 44. However, the presence of the marked white stone here makes this a bad result for Black.

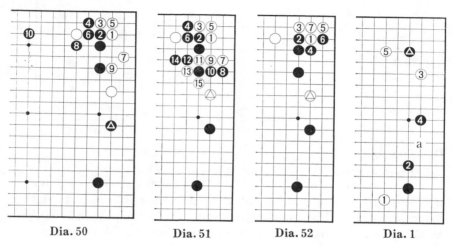

Dia. 50   Dia. 51   Dia. 52   Dia. 1

b) Double Approach Moves

Sometimes, immediately responding to an approach move against a star point stone might not be best — playing a pincer or occupying a big point might be better. This could give White the opportunity to make a second approach move against a black stone on the star point. In this section, we will study black techniques for handling this kind of attack.

Dia. 1 (Two approach moves)

After Black jumps to 2, White will sometimes play another approach move at 3 in the upper corner. In this case, Black 4 is the best move, since it gives Black an ideal position on the lower right side and defends his weak point of 'a'. Moreover, it is also a pincer, attacking the white stone at 3. On the other hand, it leaves the marked black stone a bit weak — White can attack it again with a second approach move, such as 5. Black has a number of ways of dealing with double approach move while efficiently using his pincer at 4.

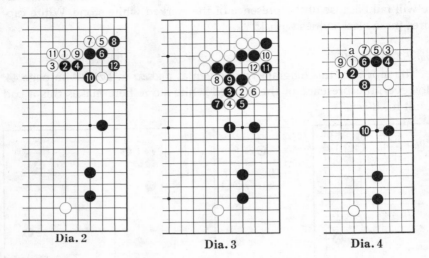

Dia. 2   Dia. 3   Dia. 4

Dia. 2 (Joseki)

Attaching at 2 is Black's usual response to the approach of White 1. This move conforms to the principle of attaching against the stronger of two attacking stones, thereby making it even stronger. Against White 3, Black draws back with 4, and White invades the 3–3 point with 5. Blocking at Black 6 is the correct direction and is consistent with his other moves at 2 and 4. After White connects at 11, Black must make the hanging connection of 12.

Dia. 3 (Black's position has collapsed)

If Black omits 12 in Dia. 2 and plays at 1 here instead, White immediately strikes at 2. Black does not made any unnatural moves, but suddenly after White 12, his position has collapsed — an inheritance from the bad shape of his stones.

See the appendix for the modern variation of the *joseki* in Dia. 2.

Dia. 4 (Variation)

Instead of first playing 3 in Dia. 2, White could immediately invade at 3. The moves to White 9 are one variation of the *joseki* in Dia. 2. As before, Black jumps into the center with 10.

It is wrong for Black force White to connect at 'a' by playing *atari* at 9. Now after Black plays at 8, White will immediately cut at 'b'. The ensuing fight will put Black at a disadvantage.

Dia. 5 (Caution)

Black must not play 6 as in this diagram. If he does, he will be in serious trouble after the cut of White 9. Black 6 in *Dia. 4* is the key move.

Dia. 6 (Overplay)

How should Black respond if White plays 4 in answer to Black 3? Black should take the key point of 5. The sequence continues to 13, and Black has secured the territory on the upper right side. White 4 is an overplay.

Dia. 7 (Black is bad)

If Black meekly responds to White 4 with 5, the sequence to Black 11 results. White gets *sente* and he can play around 'a' to squash Black's potential territory on the right side. Moreover, White has been able to use his marked stone effectively, while Black's marked stone and the one at 3 are not working at all.

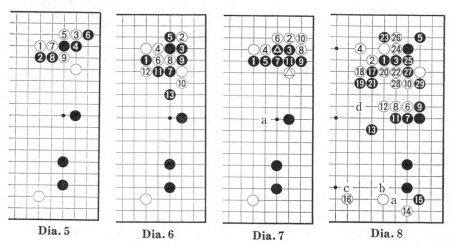

Dia. 5   Dia. 6   Dia. 7   Dia. 8

Dia. 8 (Defending the top)

When Black draws back with 3, defending at 4 is another possibility. Black must secure himself in the corner by playing on the 3–3 point. The sequence to Black 13 naturally follows. White can then safeguard his position on the lower side with 14 and 16. (If White doesn't play these two moves, Black could attach at 'a'; after White 'b', the pincer of Black 'c' will be severe on White.) Black continues by attacking the white stones above with 17 and 19, separating them from the ones on the right. The result here is very bad for White. Instead of 14 and 16, jumping to 'd' is also possible.

Dia. 9 (Double small-knight approach)

Instead of the high approach move of White 5 in *Dia. 1*, White could also play another small-knight approach at 5 as in this diagram. Black 6 is the right direction to attach ('Attach against the stronger stone!'). Some important *josekis* result from this move.

Dia. 10 (Joseki)

After Black attaches at 1, the sequence to Black 5 is the standard *joseki*. White makes an escape route to the center with 6, while threatening to push through and cut with 'a' and 'b'. Black defends with 7, 9, and 11, securing the territory in the corner. White jumps out into the center with 12, and Black 13 threatens to cut at 'c', forcing White to defend at 14. Black 15 locks up the corner and White ends in *sente*.

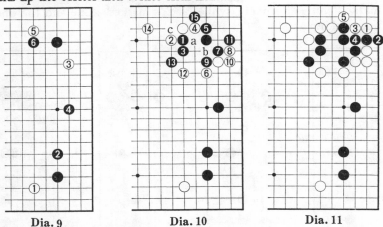

Dia. 9   Dia. 10   Dia. 11

Dia. 11 (Black is drifting in the center)

If Black doesn't play 15 in *Dia. 10*, White will clamp at 1. Black descends to 2, but White links up to the top with 5. The black stones are now drifting in the center without a base.

Dia. 12 (A bad atari)

White must not *atari* with 1. If he does, he will lose the chance to play the moves in *Dia. 11*, and Black won't have to play 15 in *Dia. 10*. White 3 now doesn't work. White 5 is no longer a threat, as Black can play the clever move of 6 to capture the white stones in the corner.

Dia. 13 (Good for Black)

If White clamps at 12, instead of jumping to 12 in *Dia. 10*, Black will descend to 13, then cut with 15. After 17, Black has a good position.

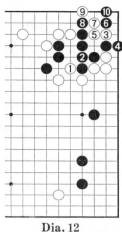

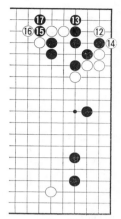

Dia. 12

Dia. 13

Dia. 14 (The diagonal extension)

White could also extend diagonally to 6. Black should simply defend at 7. After White 8, Black pincers at 9, forcing White to make a bad shape up to 12. Black takes the corner with 13, and against 16 he runs away lightly with 17.

Dia. 15 (The shoulder hit)

The shoulder hit of White 6 is another variation, Black answers by pushing up with 7. Against White 8 Black plays 9, then secures the bottom part of the right side as his territory. Finally, Black takes the corner at the top with 17 and 19, forcing White to defend with 20. Black ends in *sente*. This is a very good result for Black.

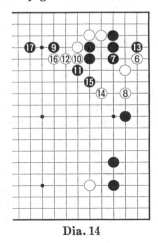

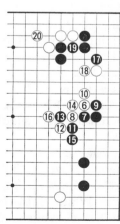

Dia. 14

Dia. 15

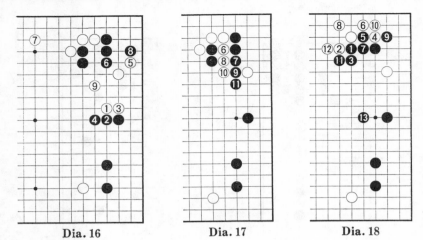

| Dia. 16 | Dia. 17 | Dia. 18 |

Dia. 16 (Overplay)

White 8 in *Dia. 15* is a bit unreasonable. What about White 3 here instead? Black simply plays 4, and the sequence to White 9 follows. Black has secured the corner with 8, has a strong position on the lower right side, and has *sente*. On the other hand, White's stones on the right are still vulnerable. From these diagrams we must conclude that the shoulder hit of 1 is an overplay.

Dia. 17 (Pushing through)

Pushing through with White 6 and 8 is also bad. In response, Black simply runs along the fourth line. He can be satisfied with the profit he has made up to 11. In contrast, White has gained very little.

Dia. 18 (Black get a big profit)

After Black 3, White could also attach at 4. The sequence to White 12 is the same like one studied in *Dia. 13* on page 21. Black concludes the sequence by jumping to 13 which takes a big profit on the right side.

Dia. 19 (White takes the corner in sente)

There is a difference, however, between *Dia. 18* above and *Dia. 13* on page 21. Because of his marked stone, White can take the corner with the moves to 5 in *sente*. Black should not omit 6 to defend his position.

Dia. 20 (The diagonal move)

The diagonal move of White 4 is another possibility. After exchanging 5 for 6, Black 7 on the 3–3 point is the only move. White plays a shoulder hit with 10. After White 16, Black moves out into the center with 17. Black's result is good, since White's stones in the center are still vulnerable.

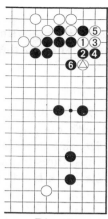

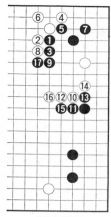

Dia. 19   Dia. 20

Dia. 21 (Black doesn't have eyes)

Black must not block with 7. If he does, White will immediately peep with 8. After 10, White's stones are secure at the top and on the right. On the other hand, Black must make eyes in the center of the board. This is why Black 7 in *Dia. 20* is the only move.

Dia. 22 (Invasion)

Invading at the 3–3 point with 4 is another variation. Black should simply block at 5. After 12, Black will jump to 13. Later on, White 'a' is *sente*, but he should not play this move immediately. Instead, he should wait until he is certain that there is no chance for his marked stone to escape into the center.

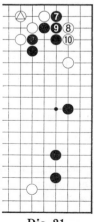

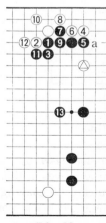

Dia. 21   Dia. 22

Dia. 23 (Sente, but —)

Instead of the connection of 10 in *Dia. 22*, White might simply connect with 10 here. In this case, Black should exchange 11 for 12 then turn at 13. White seems to get *sente*, but —

Dia. 24 (White is confined to the top)

If White doesn't respond to Black 13 in *Dia. 23*, Black can utilize the marked stone to confine White to the top with the sequence to 9. Although White will probably not play as docilely as here, Black 1 takes the vital point. If Black is afraid of complications it suffices to play 3 at 4 and make White crawl along the third line, while Black builds up powerful influence in the center.

Dia. 25 (If Black omits the exchange)

If Black omits to exchange 11 for 12 in *Dia. 23*, playing instead at 1 here, White will play 2, forcing Black 3. Now Black 'a' is answered by White 'b'. Black no longer has the confining moves in *Dia. 24*.

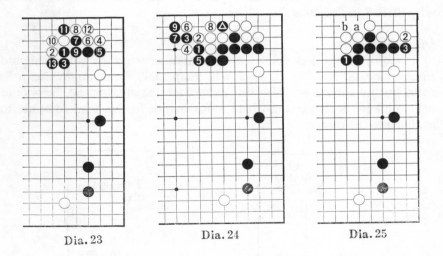

Dia. 23   Dia. 24   Dia. 25

c) Double Pincer

Dia 1 (A four-stone opening)

Look at the moves in this diagram. Black does not answer White 9 but develops quickly by playing 10. After the exchange of 11 for 12, White attacks the marked black stone a third time with 13. The question arises: can Black live in the corner?

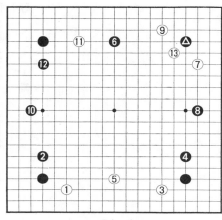

Dia. 1

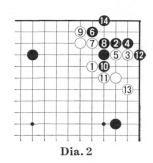

Dia. 2

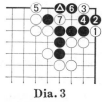

Dia. 3

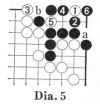

Dia. 4

Dia. 5

Dia. 2 (Black is alive)

Black can live in the corner with the moves to 14. Note that 10 and 12 are essential for Black to get two eyes.

Dia. 3 (Black dies)

Without 12 in *Dia. 2*, Black will die. After Black plays the marked stone in this diagram, White attacks with 1. The sequence continues to Black 6, but after White throws in a stone at 7, there is no way that Black can save the corner.

Dia. 4 (White cannot kill Black)

Notice how the marked black stone prevents White from killing Black. Against 1, Black 2 is the key move. White's efforts come to nothing.

Dia. 5 (White fails again)

Placing a stone on the point 1 also fails when Black takes the vital point of 2. After capturing with 6, Black can play either 'a' or 'b' to make two eyes.

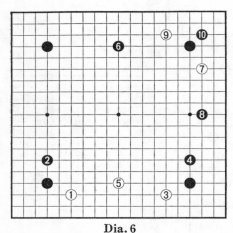

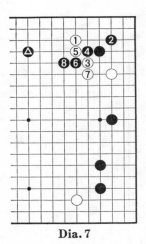

Dia. 6   Dia. 7

Dia. 6 (Another opening)

Black has played 10 on the 3–3 point. Although this strategy does not comply with the principle that Black should not allow himself to be confined to the corner, this is a strong move that should not be dismissed.

Dia. 7 (White is cut into two groups)

If White tries to confine Black with 3, Black will push through and cut with 4 and 6. We know that Black's stones in the corner are alive, so after White draws back with 7, Black will play 8. The marked black stone is on the perfect point from which to attack White 1 and 5. Furthermore, White's other three stones are weak and could come under attack later on. However, 2 should only be played when Black has the marked stone in place. Like the stone in the middle of the right side, it also becomes a pincer.

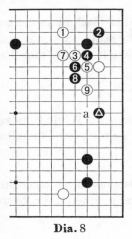

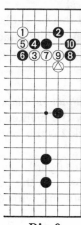

Dia. 8   Dia. 9

Dia. 8 (The ideal point)

Because the marked stone on this side is in a low position, Black should not play 4 in this direction. After Black 8, White 9 is ideally placed; the marked stone would be more effective at 'a'.

Dia. 9 (Bad for White)

If White answers 6 with 7, Black will play the moves to 10. Black will easily make life in the corner, while White will be split into two weak groups. Furthermore, the marked white stone is badly placed, forming the proverbial bad 'empty triangle'.

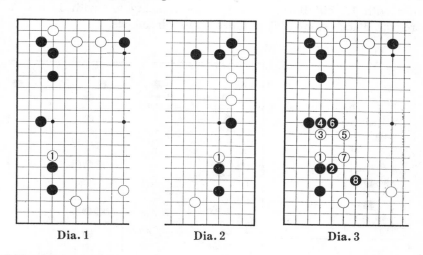

Dia. 1   Dia. 2   Dia. 3

d) The Attachment

Dias. 1 and 2 (The same attachment but different strategies)

In these two diagrams, White has attached with 1. Even though the lower parts of the black formations are similar, the surrounding positions are different. Black must choose his strategy accordingly.

Dia. 3 (The extension)

When Black is strong on the side facing the attached stone, as in *Dia. 1*, Black should respond by extending to 2. White will next play a shoulder hit at 3, and after 4 and 6, White runs away lightly with 5 and 7. Finally, Black jumps out into the center with 8. This move keeps the two white groups separated, and attacks the wide white extension at the bottom. Moreover, Black has been able to strengthen his territory on the upper left side with 4 and 6.

Dia. 4 (White descends)

White could also respond to the extension of Black 2 by descending to 3. Black will play 4, threatening to confine White to the side. Should White then slide to 5, Black will anchor himself to the corner with 6, and White may have to be satisfied with a small group on the side.

Dia. 5 (White breaks out into the center)

Black 4 only threatens to confine White to the corner. White can break out into the center with the sequence to 11. However, Black's thickness in the center after 12 will be overwhelming. White can confine Black to the corner with 13, but Black has no trouble making life with 14 and 16. Moreover, Black's stone at 12 nullifies White's influence.

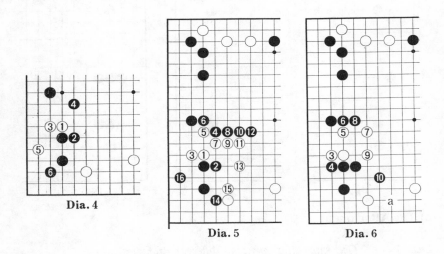

Dia. 4   Dia. 5   Dia. 6

Dia. 6 (Passive)

If Black doesn't like the variations in *Dias. 4* and *5*, he could respond to White 3 with 4, and follow the same sequence to 10 as before. However, Black 4 is a bit passive, because if we compare *Dia. 3*, Black would not play 4 but attack White at 'a' instead.

Dia. 7 (The position in Dia. 2)

Since White has a strong position on the side to back up his attaching stone at 1 in *Dia. 2*, Black must not blindly follow the *joseki* in *Dia. 3*. After Black 8, White will play 9, and the three black stones on the side are in serious trouble.

Dia. 8 (Joseki)

In this position, Black 2 is the correct response to White 1. After White blocks at 3, Black cuts with 4 and the sequence up to Black 12 is a *joseki*. Let us study these moves in more detail.

Dia. 9 (White succeeds)

Black must not connect with 4. If he does, White will also connect at 5, isolating the marked black stone.

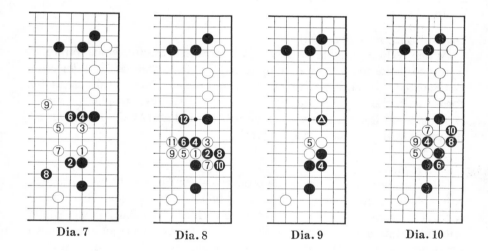

Dia. 7 **Dia. 8** **Dia. 9** **Dia. 10**

Dia. 10 (White's thickness is good)

It is also bad for Black to connect with 6 after White 5. (If the ladder is good for Black, however, this move might be possible.) Next, White *ataris* with 7 and Black connects underneath with 8 and 10. The strategic value of White's thickness in the center is much greater than Black's territory on the side. Black's position has been flattened out.

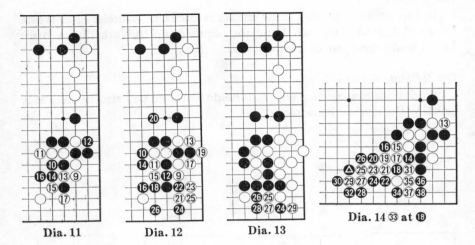

Dia. 11   Dia. 12   Dia. 13   Dia. 14 ㉝ at ⑱

Dia. 11 (White must be careful)

When White extends with 9, Black must be careful, since White is trying to make the situation complicated. If Black *ataris* at 10, then after White extends to 11, Black has no choice but play 12. Next, White takes the corner with the sequence up to 17. This result is a catastrophe for Black. His stones on the right side are overconcentrated and White has taken all the profit in the corner instead of Black.

Dia. 12 (Squeeze)

Playing *atari* from above is the proper way for Black to answer White 9. After Black connects at 12, White must block with 13. Next, Black *ataris* with 14, then plays 16, aiming to squeeze with 18. After Black makes shape with 20, White must ensure that his stones at the bottom right are alive, so he plays 21. Black 24 and 26 prevent White from linking up with his marked stone. The is an excellent result for Black, since he has a massive wall on the outside that radiates influence throughout the board.

Dia. 13 (White ends with gote)

After Black 24, White could take the corner with the moves to 29, but he ends in *gote*.

Dia. 14 (Ladder)

After White 13 in *Dia. 12*, Black can *atari* with 14 if the marked black stone is in place. If White tries to escape, all his stones will be captured with the moves to Black 38.

— 76 —

Dia. 15 (Black lives in the corner)

Playing *atari* with 9 and 11 is bad because Black's thickness in the center is too strong after 12. Furthermore, Black can live in the corner after White 13 with the moves to 20.

Dia. 16 (Variation)

If White descends to 15 in answer to 14, Black will attach at 16. White must block at 17. After the sequence to 22, Black will easily be able to make two eyes for his group.

Dia. 17 (Black's mistake)

After White 9 in *Dia. 8*, Black must not *atari* with 10 as in this diagram. White 11 would become *sente* and after White connects underneath with 13, the three marked black stones are adrift in the center without a base.

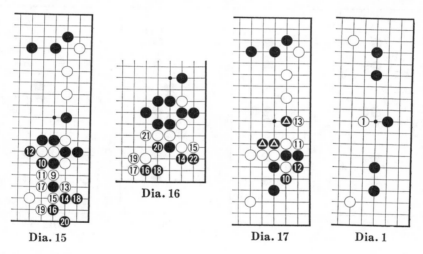

Dia. 15   Dia. 16   Dia. 17   Dia. 1

e) Capping

Dia. 1 (White caps)

The black formation on the right often appears in four- and five-stone handicap games. If Black were able to play at 1, it would be very difficult for White to invade Black's area on the right. For this reason, White would like to play in this area first, and the cap of White 1 is one of the moves at his disposal. Since Black is strong in this part of the board, White should not expect too much, and he should be satisfied if he succeeds in limiting Black's expansion. Therefore, the cap of White 1 should be regarded as an erasing move.

Dia. 2 (Bumping against the capping stone)

The safest way for Black to answer White 1 is to bump against this stone with 2. White will draw back with 3, and Black 4 and 6 are strong moves that consolidate the upper right side. White next plays 7, aiming to make influence in the center. Black should first take measures to deal with this influence, then come back and defend at 'a'.

Dia. 3 (Profit versus influence)

Instead of 7 in *Dia. 2*, White might invade with 1 as in this diagram. Black answers with 2, then cuts with 4. The sequence to White 7 follows naturally. Black next attaches at 8, and White forces his way into the center with 9 and 11. Up to Black 18, White has thickness and influence along the bottom as well as *sente* while Black has made a large profit.

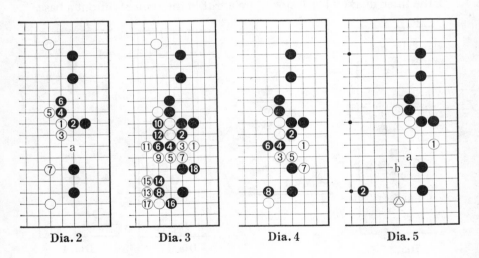

Dia. 2   Dia. 3   Dia. 4   Dia. 5

Dia. 4 (Playing lightly)

White might not like the profit Black made in *Dia. 3*. Jumping lightly to 3 is another alternative for White. After Black 8, the position isn't as defined as before, and White has many ways to continue. However, once again Black's result is good.

Dia. 5 (Leaving threats behind)

White 1 is an overplay. Black's best response is to pincer at 2, attacking the marked white stone and leaving the sequences shown in the last two diagrams as threats. If White plays at 'a', Black answers at 'b', and the marked white stone is in even greater trouble.

— 78 —

Dia. 6 (The knight move)

The standard response to a capping move at 1 is to play a knight move at Black 2. After exchanging of 3 for 4, White plays 5 as a sacrifice stone and makes a light, flexible shape with the moves up to 11. Finally, Black defend with 12. Later, he aims to attack White at 'a'.

Dia. 7 (White extends)

Instead of White 5 in *Dia. 6*, White could extend to 5 as in this diagram. Black should take the vital point of 6, and after White 9, connect underneath with 10 and 12, taking profit on the right side. In the meantime, White gets influence with 11 and 13. Note that the cut at 'a' is worth only 6 points in *gote*, so this move should not be played until the endgame.

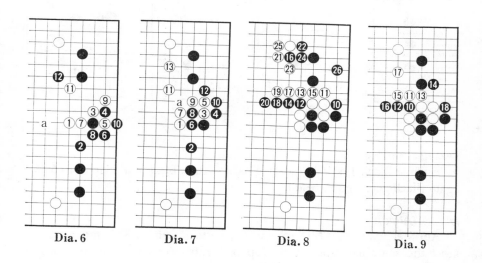

Dia. 6   Dia. 7   Dia. 8   Dia. 9

Dia. 8 (White resists)

If White resists Black 10 with 11, then Black will cut at 12. After White connects with 15, Black will attach at 16. The sequence to Black 26 naturally follows. Black is safe in the corner while White's thickness has been nullified by Black's stone at 20. In contrast, Black's influence is overwhelming.

Dia. 9 (Black cuts)

Cutting at 10 is also good for Black. The result to 18 is almost the same as *Dia. 8*. It should be obvious that White 5 in *Dia. 6* is necessary for White if he wants a satisfactory result.

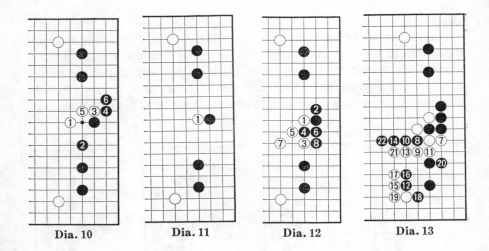

| Dia. 10 | Dia. 11 | Dia. 12 | Dia. 13 |

Dia. 10 (Drawing back)

Against Black 4, if White draws back with 5, Black will extend to 6 and again Black gets a good result.

Dia. 11 (Attaching)

Another way for White to play is to attach with 1. This move has almost the same meaning as the cap of White 1 in *Dia. 1*. It too aims at limiting Black's expansion, but it is a more direct attack.

Dia. 12 (A safe answer)

Extending to 2 is a safe way for Black to answer White's attachment at 1. The sequence continues up to 8 and Black gets the side, while White establishes a position in the center.

Dia. 13 (Bad for White)

Instead of connecting at 7 in *Dia. 12*, White can block at 7 here. Black would then cut with 8 and the sequence to Black 22 would follow. This result is bad for White. Black lives in the corner and gets thickness facing the top. Moreover, Black 22 nullifies White's thickness below.

Dia. 14 (The usual sequence)

Against White 1, Black 2 is the usual response. After connecting at 4, the open connection of 5 gives White a flexible shape. After jumping to 6, Black can aim to cap at 'a'.

Dia. 15 (White is in trouble)

If Black gets the chance to play 1, White will be in trouble. If he tries to run away with 2, Black will peep at 3 and 5, then jump to 7. White's stones are almost lost.

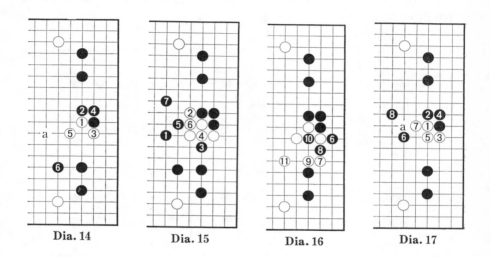

Dia. 14   Dia. 15   Dia. 16   Dia. 17

Dia. 16 (Future problems)

If Black plays 6 (instead of 6 in *Dia. 14*), White will jump lightly to 7. Up to 11 White smartly moves out into the center. This result is not really bad for Black, but his stones in the lower right could get into trouble. If he wants to keep the game simple, this way of playing is not recommended.

Dia. 17 (Unwieldy)

If White connects solidly with 5, his stones will be left with an unwieldy shape. Black will immediately attack with 6 and 8, and again White is in trouble. If White plays 7 at 'a', Black will wedge in at 7.

f) The Invasion

Dia. 1 (Invasion)

The one-space jump of Black 2 is a natural response to the approach move of White 1. When White plays his second approach move at 3 in the lower right corner, however, there are some theoretical problems with Black 4, because of its high position and the presence of White 1. A pincer at 'a' or 'd', or even a quieter move at 'b' or 'c' would be more orthodox. Of course, Black's one-space jump at 4 is not a bad move, but White 5 has become an attacking move. Since Black should not lose the initiative, his next move should also be an aggressive one. An invasion is just the move that Black had in mind when he jumped to 4.

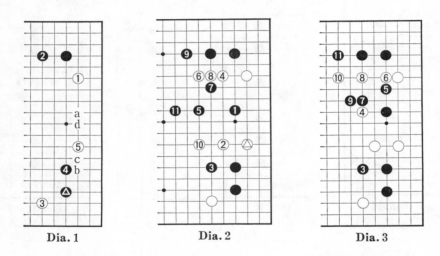

Dia. 1   Dia. 2   Dia. 3

Dia. 2 (Two weak groups for one)

Invading on the 4th line with Black 1 in answer to the marked White stone is the best move. After exchanging 2 for 3, White jumps to 4 and Black makes a two-space jump to 5. The peep of 7 helps Black defend his loose two-space formation. Finally, Black jumps to 11 and he has escaped into the center with his weak group, while all three of White's positions, at the top, in the middle and the lone stone at the bottom, are vulnerable to attack.

Dia. 3 (The cap)

If White caps with 4, Black will play a shoulder hit with 5, and after the sequence to Black 11, the result is similar to *Dia. 2*.

Dia. 4 (Shoulder hit)

If White jumps with 2 on the other side, Black can play a shoulder hit with 3, severely attacking White's lone stone. Many variations are possible, but they can only turn out well for Black.

Dia. 5 (One-space jump)

Black can also jump to 1 in answer to the marked white stone. If White defends the right side with 2, Black can severely attack White's stone below with 3 and 5.

Dia. 6 (Invading the right side)

On the other hand, if White defends the lower side by extending to 2, Black will invade deeply with 3, and after 9 White will be in trouble.

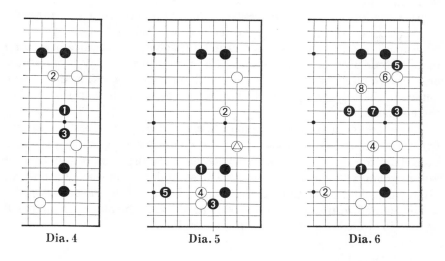

Dia. 4   Dia. 5   Dia. 6

Chapter Five

A Survey of Tesuji

A *tesuji* is a key move in a local encounter which gives the most benefi-
cial result. In chess, the term for such a move is 'brilliancy'. If your goal is
to capture a group of stones, make your own stones live, build a wall, etc.,
tesujis are the moves that help you do this. Since the encounter is usually
restricted to a small area of the board, there are not that many moves to
consider, and, in theory, you could use brute force to analyze every variation. But brute-force analysis is time-consuming. If, in a flash of insight,
you can find the *tesuji* that enables you to achieve your goal, analyzing
every variation becomes unnecessary. Once you spot the *tesuji*, the sub-
sequent moves to reach your goal often become obvious.

A *tesuji* has many forms, but it usually involves the sacrifice of a stone
or the occupation of a vital point. The opportunity to play a *tesuji* may
arise at any point in a game: in the opening during a *joseki*, in the middle
game, in killing your opponent's stones or making your own live, and in
the endgame.

There are many different kinds of *tesujis* and they are classified accord-
ing to the kind of move involved. In this chapter, we give a few examples
of each of the most important ones. Reading the first part of this chapter
will help you recognize these *tesujis*. The second part consists of problems,
arranged from easy ones to difficult ones. They can be solved using the
tesujis learned in the first part. By solving these problems, the reader will
be able to judge his progress and understanding.

1) Shortage of Liberties

More than just counting liberties is involved in capturing races. If you
can create a shortage of liberties in such situations, you will often win.

Example 1

Black has just played the marked stone, leaving White's group with
two liberties against Black's three. How can White save his five stones?

Dia. 1. White plays on the 1–2 point with 1. Notice how a black move at
'a' is impossible without first playing at 6 (because of shortage of liberties).
Hence, Black loses one liberty and White captures three stones with the
moves to 7.

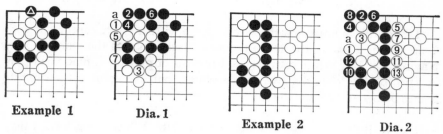

| Example 1 | Dia. 1 | Example 2 | Dia. 2 |

Example 2

The black and white groups in the corner are caught up in a capturing race. Black is far ahead in liberties, but White can win this race by creating a shortage of liberties. How does he do it?

Dia. 2. White 1 for Black 2 is a natural exchange. White 3 then gives White's group an eye. Black loses two moves since he must first play 6 and 8, but after White 13, Black can't play at 'a' because of a shortage of liberties.

| Example 3 | Dia. 3a ❹ at ① | Dia. 3b |

2) The Throw-In Tesuji

This *tesuji* involves the sacrifice of a stone. It is quite useful for saving stones outright or by creating a *ko*.

Example 3

The white stones don't have two eyes, but they are not dead yet. White has a tesuji to get the eyes he needs. Where should he play?

Dia. 3a. White throws in a stone at 1. After Black takes this stone with 2, White descends to 3. If Black continues to 6, he loses seven stones when White plays 7. Therefore, Black should simply play 4 at 7 and give up the marked stone and the one at 2, letting White get two eyes.

Dia. 3b. If White had simply descended at 1, Black would have connected with 2, and White would die in the sequence to Black 10.

Example 4

Black can save his two marked stones with a *ko* by throwing in a stone.

Dia. 4a. Black must first throw in a stone with 1. White captures it with 2, and, after 3 and 4, the *ko* starts when Black captures the stone at 2 by playing 5 at 1. If White connects at 1 instead of playing 4, Black will play 'a' and 'b'. He loses the two stones above, but he captures three white stones below and avoids the *ko*.

Dia. 4b. Black must not exchange 1 for 2. After White 4, Black can't play at 'a' because of a shortage of liberties. After 6, White will have one eye while Black has none. In a capturing race, the player not having an eye is usually at a disadvantage.

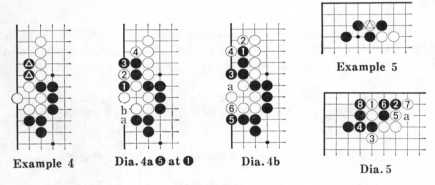

Example 4   Dia. 4a ⑤ at ❶   Dia. 4b   Example 5   Dia. 5

3) Sacrificing Two Stones Instead of One.

It is sometimes more efficient to sacrifice two stones instead of one. This *tesuji* can enable you to make good shape for your stones or it can prevent your opponent from making two eyes.

Example 5

How can White best utilize his marked stone?

Dia. 5. White should add one more stone with 1, then give them both up. He can now *atari* at both 3 and 5. After Black 6, White 7 is *sente* and Black must play at 8. Note that Black 2 is also a *tesuji*, since it leaves behind a defect in White's shape at 'a'. If Black simply plays 6 instead of 2, White would play at 2; Black 8 would then be forced, but after White played 5, he would have no defects in his shape.

If White neglects to sacrifice a stone with 1, and simply ataris at 5, Black will capture at 1. Now the white moves at 2 and 3 are no longer *sente*.

Example 6

How can Black best utilize his marked stone to repair his defect at 'a' in *sente*?

Dia. 6a. Black plays 1, sacrificing two stones. He can now defend his defect at 3 in *sente*.

Dia. 6b. If Black immediately plays 1, White will play 2 and 4 and Black ends in *gote*, since he must defend at 5.

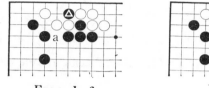

Example 6

Dia. 6a

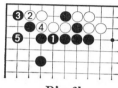

Dia. 6b

Example 7

Black has just *ataried* with the marked stone. How can White save his two marked stones and capture all the black stones in the corner?

Dia. 7a. White sacrifices two stones by descending to 1. After White ataris at 3, Black must take the two stones with 4. Next —

Dia. 7b. White throws in a stone with 5, then connects at 7, making it impossible for Black to win this capturing race. Instead of 8, Black could play at 9, but the result would be the same when White plays at 'a'.

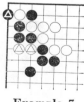

Example 7

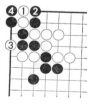

Dia. 7a

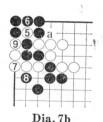

Dia. 7b

4) Linking up with the Knight Move

This is a special technique used to connect seemingly isolated stones. The knight move refers to the shape made by the two stones shown in the Reference Diagram.

Reference Dia.

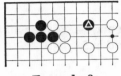

Example 8

Dia. 8a

Example 8

It seems as if the marked black stone is lost. However, Black can save it and destroy White's territory at the top.

Dia. 8a. The knight move of 1 is the *tesuji* that enables Black to link up all his stones. If White descends to 2, Black will cut with 3. On the other hand, if White plays 2 at 3, Black will play 3 at 2.

Dia. 8b. If Black unthinkingly cuts with 1, White will play 2 and 4, taking at least ten points of profit at the top.

Example 9

How can Black link up his two marked stones with his group above.

Dia. 9. The knight move of Black 1 is the *tesuji*. If White plays 2, Black simply draws back with 3 and his stones are securely linked up. Confirm for yourself that White has no way to prevent Black from linking up after Black 1.

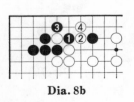

Dia. 8b

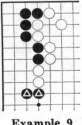

Example 9

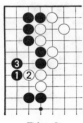

Dia. 9

5) Descending to the Edge of the Board

Depending on your orientation, a descending move may look like an ascending move, but in go it refers to a move which extends toward the edge of the board. The main use of this *tesuji* is to increase the number of liberties of your stones when they are involved in a capturing race.

Example 10

In this capturing race at the top, Black has three liberties against four for White. Yet Black has a *tesuji* that will kill the white stones.

Dia. 10. The *tesuji* is for Black to descend to 1. White can't attack Black's four stones in the corner from either direction because of a shortage of liberties. He must first connect at 6 before he can play the final *atari*, but this enables Black to *atari* first at 7. If Black plays 'a' instead of 1, White plays at 1 and it become a *ko*.

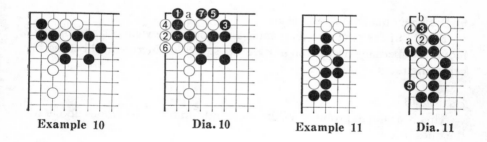

Example 10   **Dia. 10**   **Example 11**   **Dia. 11**

Example 11

Again it seems as if Black's three stones above are lost. However, he has a *tesuji* that will save these stones and capture four of White's.

Dia. 11. Descending to Black 1 is the *tesuji*. After White 2 and 4, Black plays 5, and White is left with no attacking move because he is short of liberties. If Black plays 5 at 'a', capturing the white stone, White plays 'b' and a *ko* results.

Example 12

How can White save his marked stone and capture the two marked black stones?

Dia. 12. Descending with both White 1 and 3 are the *tesujis*. After White 3, Black must play 4, so White will have enough liberties to play 5 and capture the two black stones. If Black plays at 'a' instead of 4, White will atari at 'b', Black 4, White 'c', putting the black stones in *atari*.

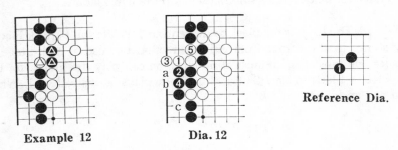

Example 12   Dia. 12   Reference Dia.

6) The Diagonal Extension Tesuji

Black 1 in the reference diagram is a diagonal extension. As a tesuji this move is especially useful for linking up stones or increasing liberties in capturing races.

Example 13

This is a simple problem. White must link up his three stones above to the ones below.

Dia. 13. There are two ways for White to link up: either the diagonal move at 1 or at 'a'. If White plays either of these two moves, it will be impossible for Black to isolate White's stones above.

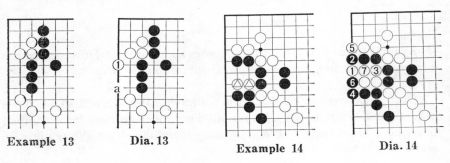

Example 13   Dia. 13   Example 14   Dia. 14

Example 14

How can White save his two marked stones?

Dia. 14. The diagonal move of White 1 is the *tesuji*. If Black tries to prevent White from linking up by descending to 2, White will cut at 3 and Black loses three stones with the moves to 7. Therefore, Black should connect at 3 after White plays 1, allowing White link up underneath at 2.

Example 15

How can Black play to take full advantage of this situation?

Dia. 15. After Black *ataris* at 1, the diagonal move of Black 3 is the *tesuji*. After the moves to 6, White is still not completely alive because of the threat of a *ko* at 'a'. If Black simply captures two stones by playing 'b', this threat would not be left behind and White would live unconditionally.

Example 16

Can Black capture the five marked stones?

Dia. 16. The diagonal move of Black 1 is the *tesuji*. If White *ataris* with 2, Black connects with 3 and White finds himself short of liberties above and below.

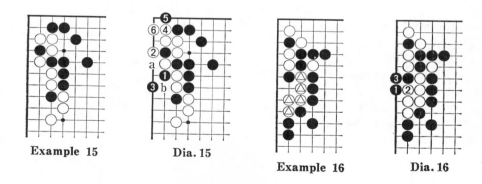

Example 15   Dia. 15   Example 16   Dia. 16

7) The Attachment Tesuji

An attaching *tesuji* is a move which directly attaches against an isolated enemy stone. This *tesuji* has a large variety of uses: killing enemy's stones, saving your own stones, making effective shape, strengthen your stones, etc.

Example 17

A life and death struggle is going on between the black and white stones. Black must attack White directly if he hopes to come out on top. Where is Black's *tesuji*?

Dia. 17. Attaching at Black 1 is the *tesuji*. After White 2, Black squeezes with the moves to 7. The fight is over when Black ataris at 9.

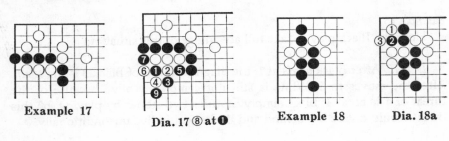

Example 17

Dia. 17 ⑧ at ❶

Example 18

Dia. 18a

Example 18

Where is the *tesuji* that enables White to capture the two black stones in the corner?

Dia. 18a. Attaching at the 2–2 point is the right move. After White 3, Black has no way to avoid being captured.

Dia. 18b. If White simply turns at 1, after White 9 the life and death of the stones in the corner will be decided by a *ko*.

Example 19

How can Black capture the two marked stones?

Dia. 19. Black should attach at 1. If White resists with 2, Black will play 3 and 5, capturing all the white stones. Therefore, White's best move is to play 'a', allowing Black to capture two stones with 2.

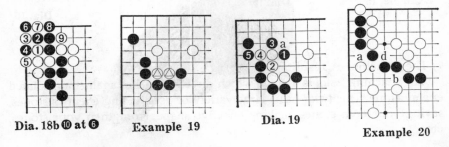

Dia. 18b ❿ at ❻

Example 19

Dia. 19

Example 20

Example 20

Black seems to be in serious trouble. White is threatening to cut at both 'a' and 'b'. If Black connects at 'a', White will play 'c', Black 'd', and White 'b', capturing all the black stones in the corner. Fortunately, Black has a *tesuji* which enables him to escape.

Dia. 20. Attaching at 1 enables Black to connect at 5 in *sente*. After White 6, Black also has time to connect at 7. If White plays 6 at 7, Black will capture a stone at 'a', making two eyes on the side.

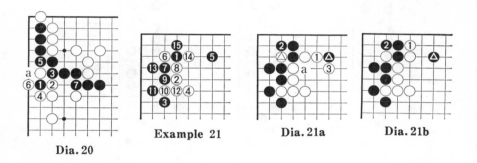

Dia. 20

Example 21

Dia. 21a

Dia. 21b

Example 21

This is an example from a *joseki*. After Black descends to 15, how should White play to make his stone at 6 work most efficiently?

Dia. 21a. White should attach against the marked black stone with 1. Black must now capture the marked white stone with 2. White now makes good shape with 3; he no longer has to worry about a cut at 'a'.

Dia. 21b. White 1 is a crass move. There is no question that this result is inferior to *Dia. 21a*. Even though he has sente, White has no effective continuation in this part of the board. The marked black stones is a thorn in his side.

Example 22

This example is a bit difficult. Black has a *tesuji* which will enable him to capture the four marked white stones.

Dia. 22a. Attaching at 1 enables Black to catch the four white stones. After White 2, Black jumps to 3 and the four white stones cannot escape.

Dia. 22b. White might draw back with 2, but after Black 3 he must jump to 4 because Black is threatening to play 'a', taking all the stones on the right side. Next Black plays 5 and 7, capturing four white stones.

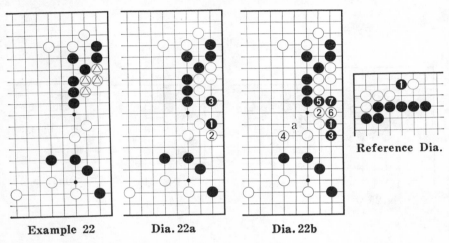

Example 22   Dia. 22a   Dia. 22b   Reference Dia.

8) Attaching at the Waist of the Knight Move

There is a proverb which says, 'Attach at the waist of a knight move!' Black 1 in the reference diagram is an example of this move. This *tesuji* is used to separate the enemy's stones, leaving them open to attack.

Example 23

Where is the vital point that will give Black the advantage?

Dia. 23. Attaching at the waist of the knight move with Black 1 is the tesuji. After Black 7, White can't defend all his weaknesses. He must either lose the three marked stones marked or the two under *atari* by Black 7. if White plays 8 at 'a', Black will play at 'b', and vice versa.

Example 24

Black has a move that can gain him the advantage.

— 94 —

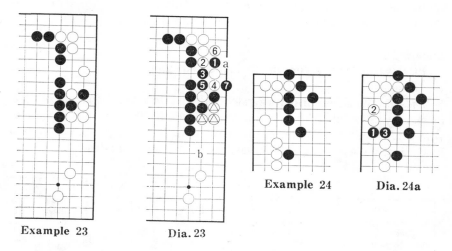

Example 23　　　　Dia. 23　　　　Example 24　　　Dia. 24a

Dia. 24a. Black 1 is the *tesuji*. White must draw back with 2 in order to live in the corner. After Black 3, White's stones have been separated.

Dia. 24b. If White tries to cut 1 off with 2, Black will clamp with 3. The four white stones in the corner are lost after Black 5.

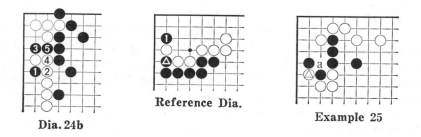

Dia. 24b　　　　Reference Dia.　　　　Example 25

9) The Clamp Tesuji

We just saw an example of the clamp *tesuji* in *Dia. 24b*. The reference diagram shows another: Black 1 together with the marked stone.

Example 25

White has just *ataried* with the marked stone. Black's first instinct might be to connect at 'a' in *gote*. However, Black has a *tesuji* which will enable him to limit White's gain in the corner and keep *sente*.

Dia. 25. The clamp of Black 1 forces White to connect with 2. Black is now free to play elsewhere. If White later captures with 4, Black plays 5, so White can't gain anything in the corner. This example shows that you should not automatically connect when faced with *atari.*

Example 26
Black's task is to capture the three marked stones.

Dia. 26. The clamp of Black 1 catches the white stones. If White plays 2, Black plays 3. White tries to run away with 4, but Black throws in a stone with 5 and captures White on the next move. If White plays 2 at 5, then Black simply plays 3 at 4. Either way, the white stones are dead.

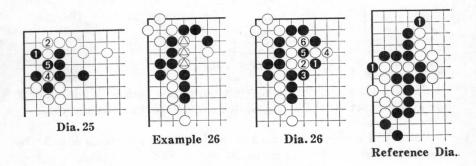

Dia. 25

Example 26

Dia. 26

Reference Dia.

10) The Hane Tesuji

A *hane* is a diagonal move from friendly stones played in contact with an enemy stone. It is a difficult word to render into English, so we will use it as an English word, the way we do for words like *tesuji, atari,* etc. Some examples are perhaps the best way to clarify what kind of move it is. In the reference diagram, each Black 1 is both referred to as a *hane.* The *hane tesuji* is very important. There are at least three go proverbs about this move: 'There is death in the *hane!*'; 'At the head of two stones play *hane!*'; and 'At the head of three stones play *hane!*' A *hane* can be very effective in a capturing race, when the number of liberties is crucial to the outcome.

Example 27
How can White link up his marked stones to the ones on the right?

Dia. 27. White should hane at 1. After cutting with 3, White sacrifices two stones by descending at 5, and then squeezes with 7, 9, and 11. Note the throw-in at 9, which is crucial to denying Black an eye. After Black connects at 12, White easily wins the capturing race. Black's best response to White 1 is to defend immediately against the cut at 7.

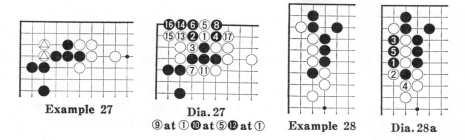

Example 27   **Dia. 27**   **Example 28**   **Dia. 28a**

⑨ at ① ⑩ at ⑤ ⑫ at ①

Example 28

White's territory on the left side may seem secure, but Black has a *tesuji* that will destroy this territory and give Black a large profit.

Dia. 28a. Black *hanes* at 1. White must cut with 2, but Black then squeezes with 3 and 5. Suddenly the corner and the left side have become Black's territory.

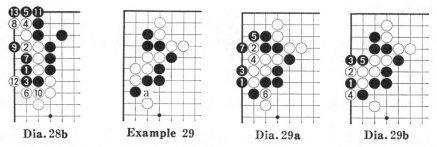

Dia. 28b   **Example 29**   **Dia. 29a**   **Dia. 29b**

Dia. 28b. White cannot connect at 2, since Black wins the capturing race with the moves to 13. White's loss here is enormous compared to *Dia. 28a*.

Example 29

White is threatening to cut at 'a', and Black's three stones in the corner seem to be lost. However, Black can capture five of White's stones.

Dia. 29a. The *hane* of Black 1 is the *tesuji*. If White resists, the moves to Black 7 capture White's stones and save the three black ones that were previously isolated.

Dia. 29b. The atari of 2 will not help White save his stones. Black again captures him with the moves to 5.

Example 30

Black is in serious trouble. If he attacks the marked white stones with 'a', White will play 'b' and capture the four black stones at the top. How should Black play?

Dia. 30a. The *hane* of Black 1 is the best move. The clamp of 2 is White's strongest response, but it's a hard move to see. The sequence to Black 7 results in a ko.

Dia. 30b. White 2 in *Dia. 30a* is a brilliant *tesuji*. If White plays 2 as in this diagram, Black will play 3 as before and capture White's three stones unconditionally.

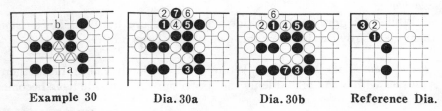

| Example 30 | Dia. 30a | Dia. 30b | Reference Dia. |

11) Two-Step Hane

Two successive *hanes*, such as Black 1 and 3 in the reference diagram, are called a two-step *hane*. This *tesuji* is often used for blocking your opponent's expansion or building up a sphere of influence.

Example 31

How should Black play in this position?

Dia. 31a. Black 1 and 3 are a good illustration of how the two-step *hane* is used to build influence and confine an opposing group of stones. After the moves to 7, Black's wall makes him strong in this area while White is confined to the corner. Cutting at 4 is important, since Black must capture this stone in a ladder. Later, White might be able to play a ladder-block to gain a move in another part of the board.

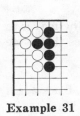
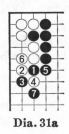
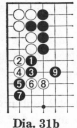
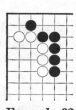

| Example 31 | Dia. 31a | Dia. 31b | Example 32 |

Dia. 31b. Extending to Black 3 is passive. If Black now *hanes* at 5 in answer to White 4, White will cut with 6, then extend to 8. This is clearly inferior for Black, compared to *Dia. 31a.* The two white stones may prove troublesome.

Example 32

This example is similar to the preceding one, except that White's position is one line higher. Will the two-step *hane* work here?

Dia. 32. Black can play the two-step *hane* with 1 and 3 and the result is similar to *Dia. 31a.*

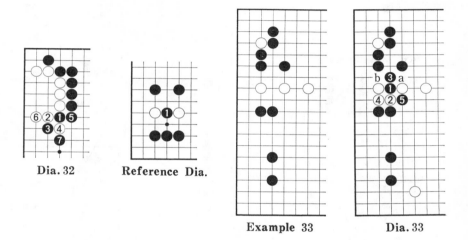

Dia. 32   Reference Dia.

Example 33   Dia. 33

12) The Wedge Tesuji

Black 1 in the reference diagram is an example of a wedge. As a *tesuji* this move often effective for separating your opponent's stones or connecting your own. It is also effective for killing or saving stones in life and death battles.

Example 33

The white stones are very weak, being sandwiched between two strong black positions. How can Black take advantage of his superior strength?

Dia. 33. The wedge of Black 1 is the *tesuji*. After Black draws back with 3, White merely compounds his loss by connecting at 4. Black cuts at 5, and White has no follow-up. If White *ataried* at 3 instead, then Black would draw back with 2, leaving two defects behind at 'a' and 'b'.

Example 34

The marked black stone seems lost, but Black has a way to save it.

Dia. 34a. Black plays 1, then wedges in with 3. Black 15 is the crucial move and the result to Black 21 is a *ko*. Cutting at 8 in answer to White 2 results in Black's failure.

Dia. 34b. If White connects at 16, the moves to 24 result, and Black captures four stones in *sente*. This is better for Black than the *ko* in *Dia. 34a*.

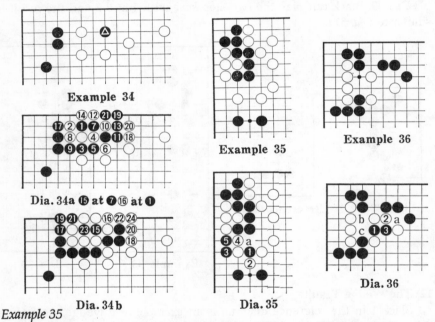

Example 34

Dia. 34a ⑮ at ❼ ⑯ at ❶

Dia. 34b

Example 35

Dia. 35

Example 36

Dia. 36

Example 35

The black group in the corner seems lost. How can Black save it?

Dia. 35. Black 1 and 3 are *atesuji*. After 5, Black saves his stones and captures four of White's besides. If White plays 2 at 'a', the result is the same.

Example 36

How can Black kill the four white stones in the corner?

Dia. 36. The wedge of Black 1 is the *tesuji*. White resists with 2, but after Black 3, White can't defend both his defects at 'a' and 'b'. If White plays at 'c' instead of 2, Black again plays 3.

Example 37

Black's group in the corner is in great danger. How can he break out into the center?

Dia. 37. Black must wedge in with 1. In answer to Black 3, White has no choice but to connect with 4. Black now captures a stone with 5 and he has escaped into the center. If White 4 at 5, Black gets a snapback with Black 4. You should confirm for yourself that the order of 1 and 3 is necessary for the success of this maneuver.

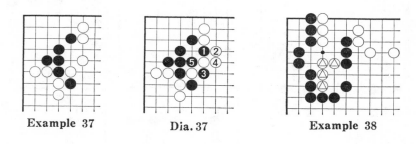

| Example 37 | Dia. 37 | Example 38 |

Example 38

How can Black capture the four marked stones?

Dia. 38a. The wedge of 1 is the move Black is looking for. White must now play 2 and 4 to save his three stones at the top.

Dia. 38b. If White resists with 2 and 4, Black will play 5, cutting off all the stones on the left. The order of 5 and 7 is not important.

Dia. 38c. Black 1 fails to capture any white stones. White will play 2 and now the wedge of Black 3 fails.

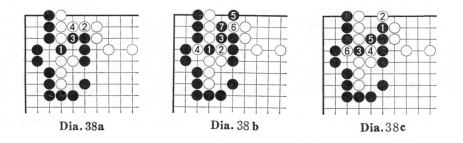

| Dia. 38a | Dia. 38 b | Dia. 38c |

Example 39

How can White kill the black stones?

Dia. 39. The wedge of White 1 is the correct answer. Black resists with 2, but White 3 and 5 stop Black from making a second eye. If Black plays 2 at 4, White would play 3 at 2, and Black can't play at 'a' because he is short of liberties. Again, Black does not get two eyes.

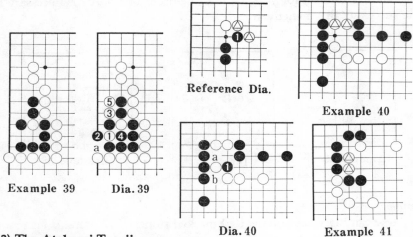

Example 39   Dia. 39

Reference Dia.

Example 40

Dia. 40   Example 41

13) The Atekomi Tesuji

Atekomi means to 'aim into'. Black 1 in the reference diagram is an example: it aims into the cavity of the two marked white stones.

Example 40

How can Black capture the two marked stones?

Dia. 40. Black 1 will capture the two white stones. White can't prevent it because he is unable to defend both of his weaknesses at 'a' and 'b'.

Example 41

How can Black capture the two marked stones and rescue his two stones in the center?

Dia. 41a. Black plays 1. If White resists with 2, Black will squeeze with 3 and 5. After White connects with 6, Black plays 7, and the fight is over.

Dia. 41b. Against Black 1, White should give up the two stones and simply draw back with 2.

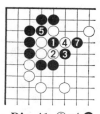

Dia. 41a ⑥ at ❶

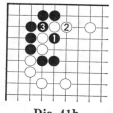

Dia. 41b

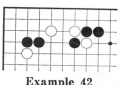

Example 42

14) The Atari Tesuji

The *atari* is a straightforward threat, but it can become a high-level tactic involving sacrifices and the evaluation of which stones are important.

Example 42

The position here resulted from a *joseki*. How can White play so as to best utilize all of his stones?

Dia. 42. White *ataris* with 1, then pushes out into the center with 3 and 5. White next takes the corner with 7. Note that the white stones on the right are discarded since White is more interested in the corner.

Example 43

Assuming that all ladders are favorable for Black, what is his best move in this position?

Dia. 43. The combination of the *atari* of Black 1 and the extension of 3 is best. Black can next play either 'a' or 'b'. That is, if White plays 'a', Black will play 'b' (capturing a stone in a ladder), and vice-versa.

Example 44

White's four stones on the left are lost, while his three at the top are weak. How can White use his lost stones to strengthen his other ones?

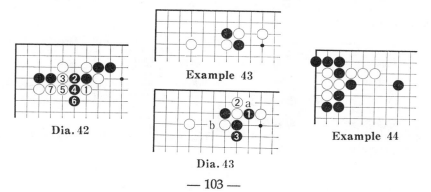

Example 43

Dia. 42

Dia. 43

Example 44

Dia. 44. The *atari* of White 1 is the *tesuji*. Up to 5, White moves out into the center gets good shape. After 6, White develops the right side with 7.

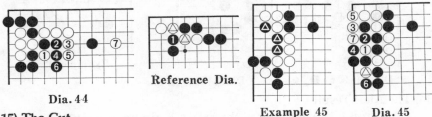

Dia. 44

Reference Dia.

Example 45   Dia. 45

15) The Cut

Black 1 in the reference diagram is an example of a cut: it separates the two marked white stones. It is usually used in combination with other *tesujis* that we have studied in the preceding sections.

Example 45

How can White save his three stones in the corner and capture the three marked stones?

Dia. 45. White 1 is an effective cut. After White 3 to 7, Black can't connect at 1 because of the marked white stone.

Example 46

Where is White's *tesuji* in this position?

Dia. 46. The cut of White 1 aims at exploiting Black's shortage of liberties. After Black 4, White again cuts with 5. This is the main point of this maneuver. After White plays 9, Black can't play at 'a' because of the presence of White 5. Instead Black must capture with 10, so White can capture two stones with 11.

Example 47

It looks as if Black's four stones in the corner are completely lost. However, Black has a *tesuji* to save them.

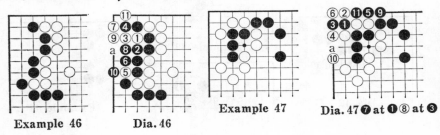

Example 46   Dia. 46   Example 47   Dia. 47 **7** at **1** ⑧ at **3**

Dia. 47. Black cuts with 1, then descends with 3, sacrificing two stones. Next, Black plays 9 and 11. White can't connect at 1, because Black will capture all his stones by playing at 'a'.

Example 48

This is a high-level problem. How should he play?

Dia. 48a. The cut of Black 1 is the *tesuji*. White next *ataris* with 2 and Black responds with 3 and 5, making a strong wall on the left side.

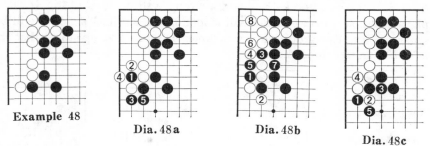

Example 48   Dia. 48a   Dia. 48b   Dia. 48c

Dia. 48b. White 2 in *Dia. 48a* is absolutely necessary. If he plays 2 as here, his loss will be large, and he will end in *gote* as well.

Dia. 48c. The average player would play the two-step hane of 1, but after Black 5, the cutting stone at 2 is bothersome. This result is clearly inferior to that of *Dia. 48a*. Playing Black 1 at 2 is too passive since this would allow White to play at 1.

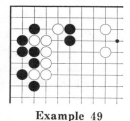
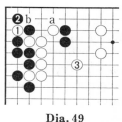

Example 49   Dia. 49

Example 49

What is White's *tesuji* in this position?

Dia. 49. Simply cutting at 1 is White's best move. If Black defends the corner with 2, White takes the territory at the top with 3. Because of the stone at 1, Black can't link up his two stones on the right with the *hane* at 'a'. If Black plays 2 at 3, White will take the corner by playing at 'b'.

16) Defending Against a Cut

When your opponent cuts or threatens to cut, the obvious move may not always be best. The following examples will show what we mean.

Example 50

White has just cut with the marked stone. How should Black defend against this cut so as to best utilize his marked stone?

Dia. 50. The *atari* of Black 1 is the correct way to defend against this cut. After 3, Black gets good shape and a strong wall on the outside. If Black plays at 2 instead of 1, White will respond at 1, so Black's stones will be separated into two groups. It is sometimes better to give up stones that are in *atari* than to defend them.

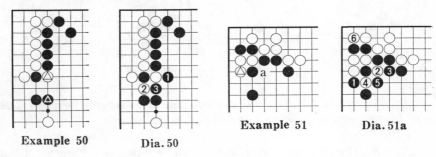

Example 50   Dia. 50   Example 51   Dia. 51a

Example 51

White has just played the marked stone, threatening a double *atari* at 'a'. How should Black defend against this threat?

Dia. 51a. The *hane* of Black 1 is the correct move. If White now *ataris* with 2, Black will *atari* with 3 and 5. White can't connect since he must first defend at 6. When Black takes the white stones at 2 and 4, his group gets good shape and two eyes. If Black simply connected at 2 instead of playing 1, White would play at 1, leaving Black with bad shape and drifting in the center without eyes.

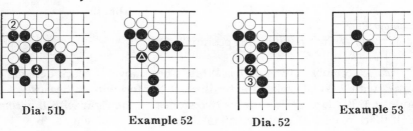

Dia. 51b   Example 52   Dia. 52   Example 53

Dia. 51b. The best way for White to answer Black 1 is to *atari* with 2. Black will play an open connection with 3. Black has good shape, but his stones are not as rock solid as before.

Example 52

Black has cut with the marked stone. White's position seems hopeless. However, he has a *tesuji* which will save all of his stones.

Dia. 52. The *atari* of White 1 is the *tesuji*. It is futile for Black to resist with 2: after White 3, Black can't attack on either side because he is short of liberties.

Example 53

Black is caught in a crosscut. How should he continue?

Dia. 53. There is a proverb which says, 'When caught in a cross-cut, extend!' Accordingly, Black extends to 1. The moves to 7 are a *joseki*.

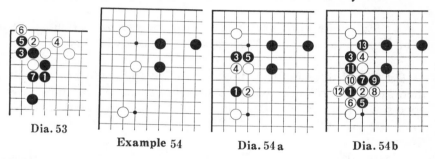

Dia. 53   Example 54   Dia. 54a   Dia. 54b

17) The Placement Tesuji

This *tesuji* is most often used to kill stones. By placing a stone on a vital point, your opponent's group will be able to make only one eye. It is also used for invading and for reducing your opponent's territory.

Example 54

How should Black attack White?

Dia. 54a. Black first places a stone at 1. If White attaches at 2, Black makes a second placement at 3. White next plays 4, and after 5 Black's invasion has succeeded.

Dia. 54b. If White blocks with 4 in answer to 3, Black will *hane* at 5. The moves up to Black 13 follow. White's loss is larger than in *Dia. 54a*.

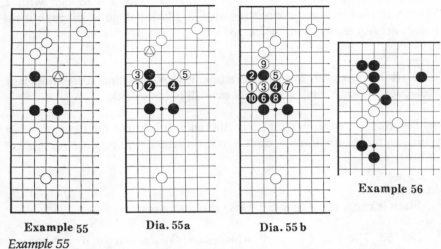

Example 55　　**Dia. 55a**　　**Dia. 55 b**

Example 56

Example 55

Considering the marked stone, where is White's best move?

Dia. 55a. White 1 is the *tesuji*. Black answers with 2 and White links up to his marked stone with 3. White next answers Black 4 with 5.

Dia. 55b. If Black blocks with 2, White will add another stone with 3, then sacrifice two stones with the sequence to 10. White ends up with good shape in the center, while Black's stones are overconcentrated.

Example 56

Where is Black's *tesuji*?

Dia. 56. Black 1, followed by 3, is the *tesuji*. White 4 is forced, but after 6, Black expands his territory in the corner and ends with *sente*. On the other hand, White's group has only one eye and will come under attack. If White plays 2 at 4, Black will play at 2 and link up with his marked stone. If White 4 at 5, Black cuts at 6 and wins.

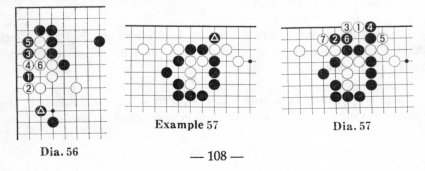

Example 57　　**Dia. 57**

Dia. 56

Example 57

Black has just played the marked stone to increase the liberties of his group and capture the four isolated white stones. How should White respond?

Dia. 57. The placements of White 1 and 3 are the only moves for White. After White 7, Black's stones are lost.

Example 58

Here's a situation which frequently occurs. Black wants to capture the three white stones in the corner.

Dia. 58. The placement of Black 1 at the 1–2 point is the *tesuji*. White loses the capturing race with the moves to Black 7.

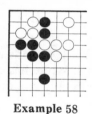

Example 58

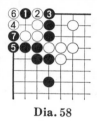

Dia. 58

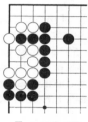

Example 59

Example 59

How can Black turn the corner into a *ko*?

Dia. 59a. The placement of Black 1 at the 1–2 point is the *tesuji*. White must connect at 2, and after Black 5 a *ko* results when White plays 6.

Dia. 59b. If White resists with 2, Black sacrifices three stones with 3 and 5. After Black 7, White is unconditionally dead.

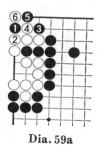

Dia. 59a

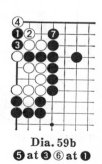

Dia. 59b
5 at **3** ⑥ at **1**

18) The Peep Tesuji

Black 1 in the reference diagram is an example of a peep. This move threatens to cut at 'a'. White must defend or his stones will be cut into two. This tesuji is often used to destroy the enemy's eyes.

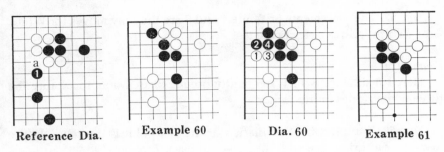

Reference Dia.   Example 60   Dia. 60   Example 61

Example 60

What is the best way for White to attack Black's group?

Dia. 60. Sliding to White 1 peeps at the point 4. If Black defends with 2, White peeps again at 3, and Black must defend with 4. White has gained profit and still has *sente*, while Black's group is left with only one eye, and becomes a target of attack.

Example 61

How should White attack the black group?

Dia. 61. White first *hanes* at 1, forcing Black to extend to 2. Next White peeps at 3, leaving the black group eyeless and drifting in the center of the board.

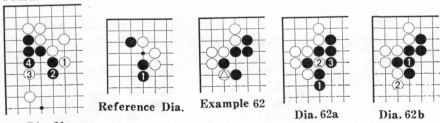

Dia. 61   Reference Dia.   Example 62   Dia. 62a   Dia. 62b

19) Extending

Black 1 in the reference diagram is an example of an extension. This kind of move is not very spectacular, but sometimes when your stones are under attack it becomes the perfect defensive move for securing good shape.

Example 62

How should Black answer the *atari* of the marked white stone?

Dia. 62a. Black should give up a stone and extend to 1. After White takes with 2, Black blocks with 3, making a strong wall facing the center.

Dia. 62b. Connecting at Black 1 would be a bad move. Next, White would extend to 2. The difference between this and *Dia. 62a* is obvious.

Example 63

How should White answer the marked black stone?

Dia. 63. Black 1 destroys the eye at 'a', so White must be careful how he answers. Extending 2 is the best move, since it makes good shape.

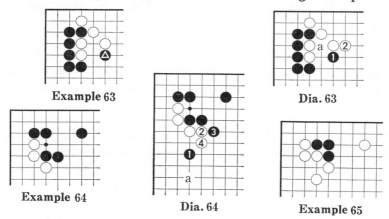

Example 63

Dia. 63

Example 64

Dia. 64

Example 65

20) Miscellaneous Tesuji

Here are a few more *tesujis* that you will probably come across. We will give one example of each.

Example 64

How should Black attack the white stones?

Dia. 64. The pincer of Black 1 is the *tesuji*. After White 2, Black hanes at 3, forcing White to make bad shape. Black could also play 1 at 'a'. The choice depends on the situation in other parts of the board.

Example 65

Black is under attack. How can he best defend his stones?

Dia. 65. The one-space jump of 1 is Black's best move. Depending on how White plays, Black can make good shape by playing either 'a' or 'b'.

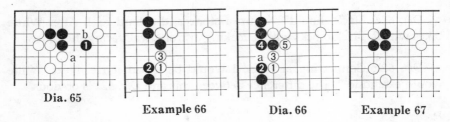

Dia. 65   Example 66   Dia. 66   Example 67

Example 66

White forces with 1 and extends to 3. How should Black answer?

Dia. 66. Black should connect at 4. If he plays at 'a' instead, White would *atari* at 5, and Black would have to respond by playing 4, ending in *gote*.

Example 67

There is a go proverb which says, 'In a symmetrical position, play on the central point!' Here is a position in which White can put this proverb to use.

Dia. 67. White plays a diagonal move at 1, on the central point of this position. If Black descends to 2, White will play 3, or vice versa. By playing on the central point, White creates two threats, but his opponent can defend against only one of them.

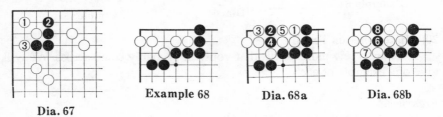

Dia. 67   Example 68   Dia. 68a   Dia. 68b

Example 68

This problem uses a technique called 'under the stones'. You would be quite a strong player if you were to read out a position such as this in a game. How can White make two eyes for his stones?

Dia. 68a, b and c. White begins by playing 1 and Black plays 2 on the vital point. Black sacrifices two stones, then throws in a stone at 6, putting four white stones and a single white stone below 6 into *atari*. The surprising move is White 7. White gives up four stones, but when Black captures with 8, White *ataris* with 9, then takes two stones with 11. His group in the corner now has two eyes.

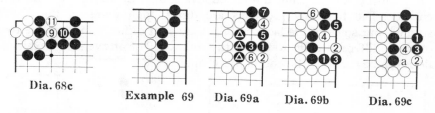

Dia. 68c   Example 69   Dia. 69a   Dia. 69b   Dia. 69c

Example 69

Where is the vital point that will enable Black to save his stones?

Dia. 69a. There is a proverb which says, 'The center of three stones is the vital point.' Black 1, a one-space jump from the center of the three marked stones, is the only way Black can make two eyes for his stones. White's efforts to kill Black are useless.

Dia. 69b. Black 1 is not a good move. White plays at the vital point of 2 (the center of the three stones), and after White 6, Black can't attack from either direction because he is short of liberties.

Dia. 69c. If Black defends with 1, White plays 2, threatening to occupy the vital point at 3. But as soon as Black plays 3, White robs Black of his second eye by playing 4. Black can't play at 'a' because he is short of liberties.

Tesuji Problems

This section consists of 50 problems arranged in order of difficulty. They can be solved using the techniques shown in the first part of this chapter. The first few problems are direct applications of the *tesujis* studied, but some of the later problems are a bit difficult and involve two or three different *tesujis* to obtain the solution. The answers and explanations can be found at the end of this chapter.

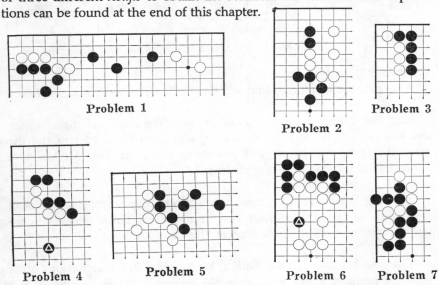

Problem 1

Problem 2

Problem 3

Problem 4

Problem 5

Problem 6

Problem 7

Problem 1. Expand Black's territory, reduce White's, and keep *sente*.

Problem 2. Black to link up his two groups.

Problem 3. Black to confine White to the corner and build up influence on the outside.

Problem 4. Black's marked stone is attacking White's stones above. Where is the vital point for White to make good shape?

Problem 5. What is White's *tesuji* here?

Problem 6. Black to link up his marked stone to his stones at the top.

Problem 7. White to kill the four black stones.

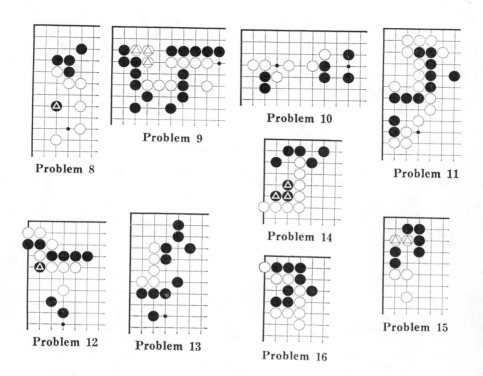

Problem 8

Problem 9

Problem 10

Problem 11

Problem 14

Problem 15

Problem 12

Problem 13

Problem 16

Problem 8. Black to link up his marked stone to the ones above.

Problem 9. How can Black capture the three marked white stones?

Problem 10. How can Black make good shape for his stones at the top?

Problem 11. How can Black save his five stones on the left side?

Problem 12. Black has just cut with the marked stone, threatening to cut off the white group below. How can White save his stones?

Problem 13. Black to kill White.

Problem 14. How can White capture the three marked stones?

Problem 15. White to link up his two marked stones to the ones below.

Problem 16. How can Black capture three stones and save his own?

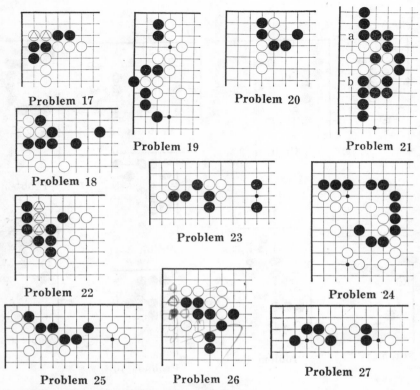

Problem 17

Problem 18

Problem 19

Problem 20

Problem 21

Problem 22

Problem 23

Problem 24

Problem 25

Problem 26

Problem 27

Problem 17. Black to capture the marked white stones.

Problem 18. Black to capture the three white stones in the corner.

Problem 19. How can Black link up with his two stones in the corner?

Problem 20. White to capture the two black stones in the corner.

Problem 21. White can play at either 'a' or 'b' to make two eyes. How can Black prevent this and kill the white stones?

Problem 22. White to save his marked stones and capture all Black's.

Problem 23. How can Black gain the advantage here?

Problem 24. Can Black save his three endangered stones?

Problem 25. Where is the vital point for White in this position?

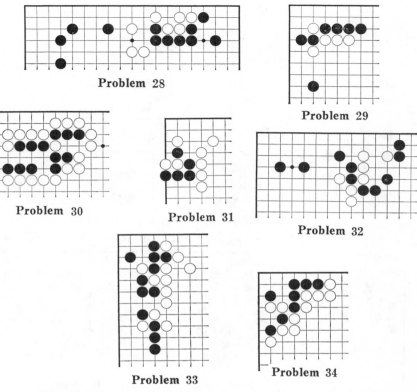

Problem 28

Problem 29

Problem 30

Problem 31

Problem 32

Problem 33

Problem 34

Problem 26. How can White link up all of his stones?

Problem 27. White has a *tesuji* which makes his stones work efficiently.

Problem 28. Black can gain the upper hand in this position.

Problem 29. How can White give his stones on the outside good shape?

Problem 30. White has a *tesuji* which will kill the black stones.

Problem 31. How can Black gain the upper hand in the corner?

Problem 32. White to save his four isolated stones at the top.

Problem 33. White can break into Black's territory on the side.

Problem 34. White to kill the black stones in the corner.

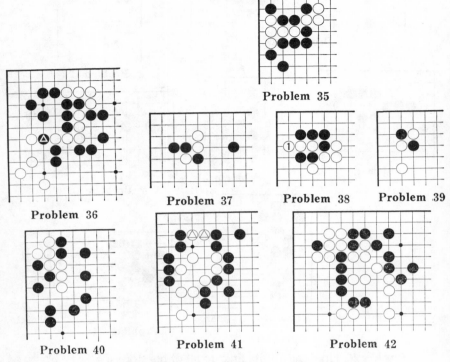

Problem 35

Problem 36

Problem 37

Problem 38

Problem 39

Problem 40

Problem 41

Problem 42

Problem 35. White has a *tesuji* that can turn the corner into a *ko*.

Problem 36. When Black plays the marked stone, he seems to have caught the five white stones. However, White has a way to save them.

Problem 37. How can White give his two stones at the top good shape?

Problem 38. How should Black respond when White descends to 1?

Problem 39. What is Black's best move in this position?

Problem 40. White's stones in the corner can live in a *ko*.

Problem 41. Black to play and capture the two marked stones.

Problem 42. Black's six stones are in danger. How can Black save them?

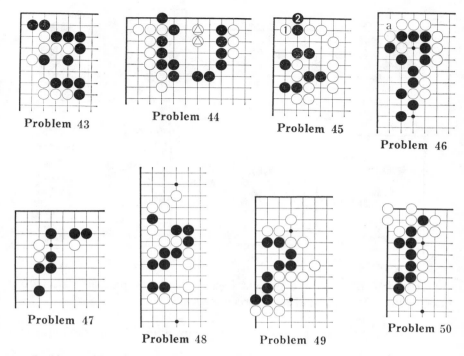

Problem 43

Problem 44

Problem 45

Problem 46

Problem 47

Problem 48

Problem 49

Problem 50

Problem 43. Black can capture four white stones in the corner with a *ko*.

Problem 44. White to save his two marked stones.

Problem 45. In answer to the clamp of White 1, Black has descended to 2. How can White take advantage of this mistake?

Problem 46. Black is threatening to cut at 'a'. How does White defend?

Problem 47. How can White make inroads into Black's corner?

Problem 48. Black has a brilliant *tesuji* with which to rescue his six stones on the left.

Problem 49. White to kill the black stones.

Problem 50. How can Black create a *ko*, thereby saving his stones?

Answers to Tesuji Problems

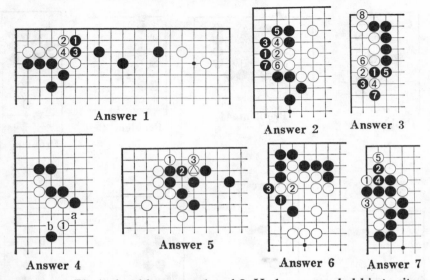

Answer 1

Answer 2   Answer 3

Answer 4

Answer 5

Answer 6   Answer 7

Answer 1. Black should peep at 1 and 3. He has expanded his territory and reduced White's, and he still retains *sente*.

Answer 2. Black links up both of his groups with 1. White can't stop it.

Answer 3. Black 1 and 3 confine White to the corner and give Black a wall that gives him a lot of strength in the center. After 7, White must descend to 8 to make two eyes for his group. Black ends in *sente*.

Answer 4. White 1 is the best move. White can make good shape by playing at either 'a' or 'b'.

Answer 5. White 1 and 3 save the marked stone because Black is short of liberties. If White plays 1 at 2, Black plays at 1 and capture two stones.

Answer 6. Black clamps at 1. White can't stop Black from linking up his stones with 2, so his territory here is destroyed. If White tries to prevent Black from linking up by descending to 3 instead of connecting at 2, Black will capture two stones by playing at 2, making a larger profit.

Answer 7. White attaches at 1 and the black stones die in the sequence to White 5.

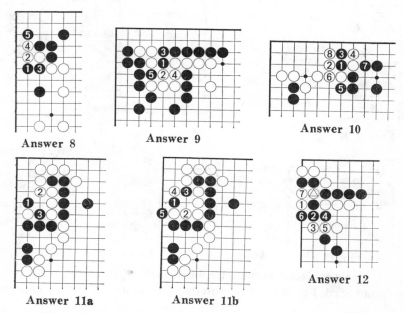

Answer 8

Answer 9

Answer 10

Answer 11a

Answer 11b

Answer 12

Answer 8. Black can link up his positions by playing the knight move of 1. It is futile for White to resist by playing 2 and 4, since Black captures three stones when he plays 5.

Answer 9. Black wedges in with 1, leaving cutting points at 4 and 5. White can't defend them both, so White must answer 3 with 4. Black then cuts off three stones in the corner. If White plays 2 at 3, Black will play 2.

Answer 10. Black first cuts with 1, then descends to 3. Next, Black sacrifices these two stones, using them to make good shape on the outside with 5 and 7. White must answer with 8, so Black ends in *sente*.

Answer 11a. Black clamps at 1 and White must connect at 2. Black next catches a stone with 3, making two eyes for his group.
Answer 11b. If White connects at 2, Black cuts at 3. If White next *ataris* at 4, Black plays 5, and the five white stones are trapped: White can't capture the black stone at 3 because Black will recapture at 3 in a 'snapback'.

Answer 12. White ataris at 1 and Black can't capture White at 7 because of a snapback. After Black extends to 2, White attaches at 3. The moves to White 7 show that further resistance is useless.

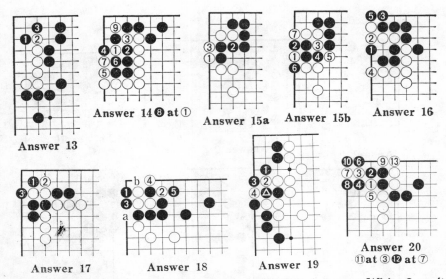

Answer 14 ⑧ at ①

Answer 15a   **Answer 15b**   **Answer 16**

Answer 13

Answer 17   **Answer 18**   **Answer 19**

Answer 20
⑪ at ③ ⑫ at ⑦

Answer 13. Black 1 is the only way to kill White's group. White 2 can't separate Black 1 from his group on the right, since 3 ensures a link-up.

Answer 14. By attaching at the waist of the knight move with 1, White aims to catch Black short of liberties after he connects at 8.

Answer 15a. The *hane* of 1 is the *tesuji* that enables White to link up. Black must connect at 2, so White links up with 3.

Answer 15b. If Black tries to keep White separated with 2, White pushes through with 3, and the black stones will be short of liberties after White 7.

Answer 16. Black plays the diagonal move of 1 and captures White with the sequence to 5.

Answer 17. Black attaches with 1. After 3, White can't save his three stones. If White 2 at 3, Black 3 at 2, and White's stones will be captured.

Answer 18. Black attaches at 1 and White is dead after Black plays 5. If White plays 2 at 3, Black will atari at 'a', then connect at 2, so White is still dead. On the other hand, if White plays 2 at 'a', Black 3 will play at 'b'.

Answer 19. The diagonal extension of 1 enables Black to link up his two groups. Black then plays 3, allowing White to capture two stones with 4, but Black recaptures where the marked stone was, so he has linked up.

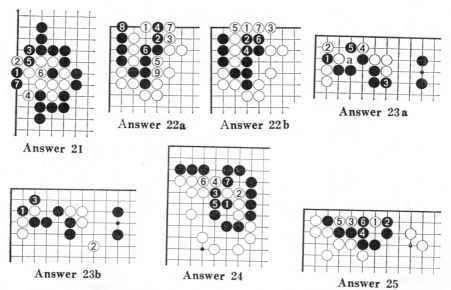

Answer 21

Answer 22a   Answer 22b

Answer 23a

Answer 23b   Answer 24

Answer 25

Answer 20. White plays 1 and 3, then sacrifices the stones at 3 and 7. White then throws in a stone with 11 and connects at 13. Black is dead.

Answer 21. This is a symmetrical position, so Black plays on the central point of 1. After Black 7, the white stones are dead.

Answer 22a. The diagonal extension of White 1 is the *tesuji* to capture the black stones. After White 7, Black finds himself short of liberties.
Answer 22b. Against Black 2, White 3 is the correct response. White links up his stones and catches Black's with the moves to 7.

Answer 23a. Black 1 is the *tesuji*. If White plays 2, Black turns with 3, isolating the three white stones. If White tries to link up with 4, Black will block at 5. White can't play at 'a' now, because he is short of liberties.
Answer 23b. On the other hand, if White runs away with 2, Black will take the corner with 3.

Answer 24. The *atekomi* of Black 1 saves the black stones. After White connects at 2, Black wedges in with 3. Since White can't defend at both 6 and 7, Black can save his stones and capture four of White's.

Answer 25. White 1 is the *tesuji*. If Black stops White from linking up with 2, White plays 3 and 5, leaving Black with one eye.

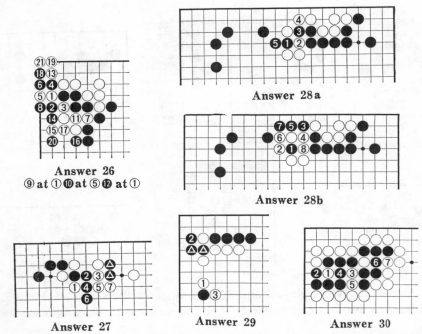

Answer 28a

Answer 28b

Answer 26
⑨at① ⑩at⑤ ⑫at①

Answer 27

Answer 29

Answer 30

Answer 26. The *hane* of White 1 is the *tesuji*. White then sacrifices two stones with 5. After Black 6, White throws in stones with 7 and 9. White wins the capturing race with the moves to 21.

Answer 27. White first *ataris* with 1, even though his intention is to gain profit on the other side. Next, White 3 and 5 force Black to answer with 4 and 6. After White 7, the marked stones are almost captured.

Answer 28a. Wedging in with Black 1 is the *tesuji*. If White responds with 2, Black will play 3 and 5. The three white stones are now drifting in the center, and the white group at the top does not yet have two eyes.
Answer 28b. If White *ataris* on the other side with 2, Black will *hane* with 3, and the moves to 7 result in the capture of the white stones at the top.

Answer 29. The attachment of White 1 threatens the two marked stones. Black must answer with 2. Next, White plays 3, giving his stones good shape and severely limiting the freedom of the black stone below.

Answer 30. White wedges in with 1. If Black plays 2, White cuts with 3 and the moves to Black 6 are forced. Black is left with only one eye.

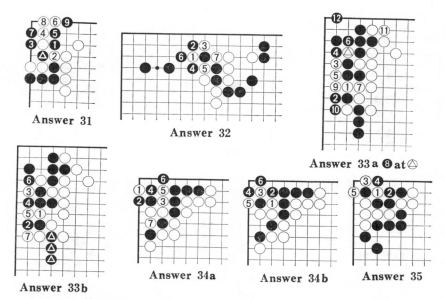

Answer 31

Answer 32

Answer 33 a ❽ at ⚪

Answer 33b

Answer 34a

Answer 34b

Answer 35

Answer 31. The *hane* of Black 1 is the *tesuji*. If White cuts with 2, Black *ataris* at 3 (White can't capture the marked stone because he is short of liberties), and there is no way for White to save his stones in the corner.

Answer 32. White attaches at 1. If Black *hanes* at 2, White cuts with 3 and the sequence to 7 is forced. White has captured two stones and his own have linked up with his allies in the center. If Black played 2 at 3, White would answer at 2 and the result would be the same.

Answer 33a. After White *ataris* at 1, the *hane* of 3 is *tesuji*. Black must play 12, ending in *gote*, so White has successfully invaded the left side.
Answer 33b. Black could block with 4 in answer to 3, but after Black 6, White can capture two stones with 7, the three marked stones are drifting without a base.

Answer 34a. The placement of White 1 results in the unconditional death of the black group.
Answer 34b. If White pushes through at 1, a *ko* will result after Black 6. If White 1 at 3, then Black 2 at 4.

Answer 35. The cut of White 1 is the *tesuji*. Black must connect with 2, and a *ko* results after White 5. If Black plays at 5 with 4, White will connect at 4, and Black can't *atari* on either side because he is short of liberties.

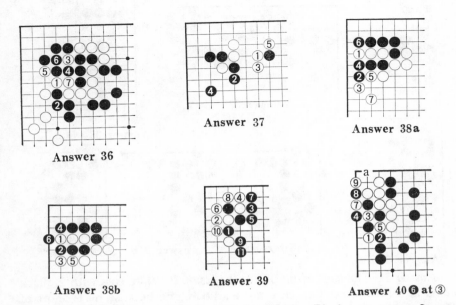

Answer 36

Answer 37

Answer 38a

Answer 38b

Answer 39

Answer 40 ❻ at ③

Answer 36. White wedges in with 1 and, after Black connects at 2, cuts at 3. Because Black is short of liberties, he can't stop White from linking up his endangered stones to the ones on the left with the moves to 7.

Answer 37. White attaches at 1 and Black must extend to 2. (White threatens to *atari* at 2, followed by White 3.) After exchanging 3 for 4, White makes good shape at the top with 5.

Answer 38a. When White descends to 1, the diagonal extension of 2 is the *tesuji*. Because of this move, White must defend at 7, ending in *gote*.

Answer 38b. If Black simply answers White 1 by blocking at 2, White will play 3 and 5, and it will be Black who ends in *gote*.

Answer 39. Black first forces with 1 and 3, then connects with 5. White has to capture the stone in the corner with 6 and 8. Next Black 9 and 11 make a strong outside wall.

Answer 40. Attaching at 1 is White's first *tesuji*. Next he throws in a stone at 3, then threatens to start a ko with 5. Black connects with 6. White again throw in a stone at 7, and after 9, Black will destroy White's eye-shape by playing at 'a'. The *ko* then begins with White 7.

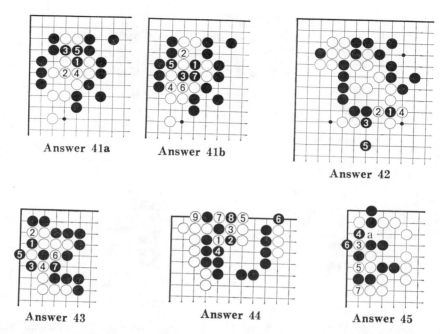

Answer 41a   Answer 41b

Answer 42

Answer 43   Answer 44   Answer 45

Answer 41a. Black wedges in with 1. White must connect at 2, but Black catches the two white stones at the top with 3 and 5.

Answer 41b. If White connects at 2, Black plays 3 and White's loss is larger than in *Answer 41a.* If White plays 2 at 7, Black will play at 6.

Answer 42. The wedge of Black 1 is a spectacular tesuji. It is the only way Black can escape. After Black 3, White must capture with 4, so Black jumps to 5, escaping into the center.

Answer 43. Black must cut with 1, then atari with 3. With the sequence to 7, Black can capture the five stones above by winning a *ko.*

Answer 44. White cuts with 1, then *ataris* at 3. Descending to 5 threatens to link up to the right, so Black is forced to play 6. White throws in a stone with 7 and, after 9, Black can't connect at 7 because he is short of liberties.

Answer 45. The cut of White 3 is the *tesuji.* After the sequence to 7, White has rescued two of his stones and captured two of Black's. If Black plays 4 at 5, White will play at 'a'.

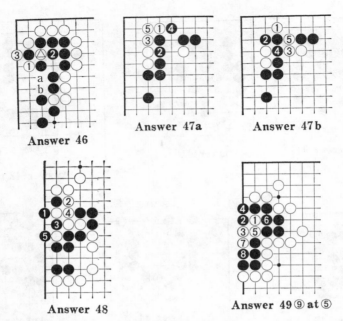

Answer 46

Answer 47a

Answer 47b

Answer 48

Answer 49 ⑨ at ⑤

Answer 46. White 1 and 3 are severe moves. They result in a *ko* that will be hard for Black to win. If Black descends to 3 instead of capturing the marked stone with 2, White will play at 'a'; after Black 2, White ataris at 'b', and Black's position is hopeless.

Answer 47a. Attaching at White 1 is the *tesuji*. If Black plays 2, White lives in the corner with 3 and 5. If White plays 1 at 3, Black would play at 1 and White's stones would die.

Answer 47b. If Black blocks at 2, White will peep at 3. Black connects at 4, and White pushes through at 5. This result is much worse for Black, since his profit on the left is small and his wall has been neutralized.

Answer 48. At first glance, Black 1 seems to be an ineffective move, but it is a *tesuji* which aims to make White short of liberties. After White 2, Black throws in a stone at 3, forcing White to connect with 4. When Black finally captures with 5, his group on the left has two eyes.

Answer 49. This is an example of the 'under-the-stones' *tesuji*. After Black captures four stones with 8, White plays at 5 with 9, capturing five stones and killing the rest.

Answer 50a. Black first throws in a stone at 1, then another at 3. After White 6, a *ko* results. White can't connect at 1 because of the presence of the marked stone.

Answer 50b. If White descends to 2, Black *ataris* four white stones with 3. White captures with 4 and when Black plays 5, White can't stop Black from getting two eyes.

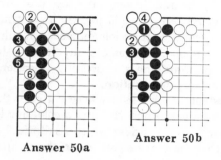

Answer 50a

Answer 50b

Chapter Six

The Endgame

The endgame is the decisive part of the game. You can take a big lead in the opening and in the middle game, but lose it in the endgame. Therefore, studying endgame technique is just as important as studying the opening and middle game. Most people, however, would rather study the opening than the endgame. Endgame study takes a lot of hard work: counting and analysis. Studying the opening is easier: you learn some general principles and rely on intuition.

The endgame usually begins somewhere between the one hundredth and two hundredth moves, when all large areas have been occupied, all large groups stabilized, and it is clear which territories belong to whom. It is in the endgame that the players cash in on their efforts in the opening and middle game and profit and loss become tangible. There is nothing easy about this stage of the game. An unskillful player who becomes confused in the tangled business of the endgame is apt to find that he has been left holding the small change, while his opponent has walked off with all the large items and has won the game.

To avoid being swindled in the endgame, you should be aware of a few basic principles, know some endgame *tesuji*, and be willing to do some counting. To start with, here is some instruction on the last of these matters.

a) Counting the Size of a Territory

Counting may seem like a nuisance in a game intended for pleasure and relaxation, but it is a necessary guide to intelligent play. Too often one sees a player who is hopelessly far behind in a game, but happily unaware of this state of affairs, playing on and on to the bitter end, wasting his own time and trying the patience of his opponent. Just as often, one sees a player who unknowingly holds a safe lead throw it away by taking badly calculated risks in search of a few extra points. All this would be avoided if the players at fault would only learn to make rough counts of their territories, and their opponents' territories, during the course of the endgame, then apply the obvious principle that if you are ahead, play safe, if you are behind, try whatever you think necessary to give yourself a chance to win; and if you can see no chance at all, resign.

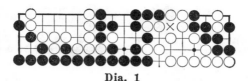

Dia. 1

Dia. 1. No doubt you already know how to count. Test yourself by glancing at this diagram and filling in the accompanying table. The x indicates a captured black stone.

	Black		White	
Right hand corner	_____	Upper left	_____	
Left side	_____	Upper right	_____	
Center	_____			

Dia. 2   **Dia. 3**   **Dia. 4**   **Dia. 5**

Black: right hand corner — zero points
No points are counted in a seki.

Dia. 2 (Black: left side — two points)
Eventually Black will have to connect at 'a', so only the two points marked x are territory.

Dia. 3 (White: upper left — eight points)
Similarly, White will eventually have to connect at 'a'.

Dia. 4 (Black: center — seven points)
Besides the five points marked X, Black should count two points for the dead stone. When the game is over, one of these two points will actually be his territory, and the other will appear as a deduction from one of White's territories. During the game it is easier and more natural to count both points together inside the territory containing the marked stone.
No point for Black at 'a', where he will eventually have to connect.

Dia. 5 (White: upper right — six points)
Just as Black counted two points at X in the last diagram, White should count two points at x where he has captured a black stone. Even though that stone is now sitting in the lid of his bowl, he should continue to identify it with the territory from which it was taken.

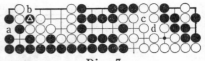

Dia. 6   Dia. 7

③, ❻, ⑨, and ⓬, ko

The reason for doing so is to stabilize the calculations of the sizes of the territories. Suppose that in the course of a *ko* fight elsewhere on the board the moves in *Dia. 6* take place, leaving the position shown in *Dia. 7*. If you fail to take account of the captured stones now removed from the board, the territories have all changed — Black is down to one point on the left side and four in the center, for example. But if you count correctly, the reckoning is just as before:

Black: left side — two points, (one for the prisoner at 'a')
center — seven points, (three prisoners plus four more points of territory)
White: upper left — eight points, (now two points at   , none at 'b')
upper right — six points, (counting prisoners at 'c' and 'd')

In ko fights, and some other situations, exchanges of prisoners take place. There you should count not the total number of stones lost by each side, but only the net difference. For example, *Dia. 8* shows a familiar position in which White has captured one stone at x. The exchange in *Dias. 9* and *10* is to be expected, Black capturing two white stones and White recapturing one black one. In the final position, shown in *Dia. 11*, you should not count two prisoners for Black and two for White, but only the difference, which is conveniently zero.

Try to form the habit of estimating the score as early as possible during in your games, counting the territories individually and keeping track of prisoners as shown above, so that your calculations will be upset as little as possible by future developments. This means that you will be faced with the problem of counting territories which, unlike the ones so far, are not completely defined. How to handle that problem is, in a way, the subject of the next section.

Dia. 8

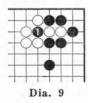

Dia. 9

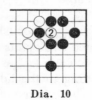

Dia. 10

Dia. 11

b) Sente Endgame

Dia. 1. White has a live group in the corner. How much territory does it contain?

Dia. 2 (White plays in gote)
If it his turn and he has nothing better to do, White can play 1, making his corner territory worth six points. He is, however, giving up his turn, so White 1 will be a good move only very close to the end of the game.

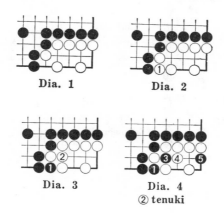

Dia. 1   Dia. 2

Dia. 3   Dia. 4
                ② tenuki

Dia. 3 (Black plays in sente)
If it is Black's turn, he can trim White down to five points by playing 1 here. He does not give up his turn, because White has to answer at 2.

Dia. 4 (White plays elsewhere)
If White fails to play 2, he risks his whole corner group.

Comparing *Dias.* 2 and 3, we see that there is one point at stake in this corner. However, long before White is willing to give up his turn to get that one point, Black should be able to find a time when he has sente, and *Dia. 4* poses an unacceptable threat to White. Then he can play *Dia. 3*, getting the one point, keeping *sente*, and then going on to something else. White had better resign himself to accepting *Dia. 3*, recognizing that if he gets a chance to play *Dia. 2*, it will have to be due to absent-mindedness on Black's part.

In short, White should count his territory in *Dia. 1* as being five points.

This kind of situation, which is very common, is called a one-sided *sente* endgame situation. Alternatively, we say that the play in *Dia. 3* is Black's *sente* endgame.

Dia. 5. This diagram abounds in *sente* endgame plays. See if you can find all of them and, by visualizing them, fill in the accompanying table.

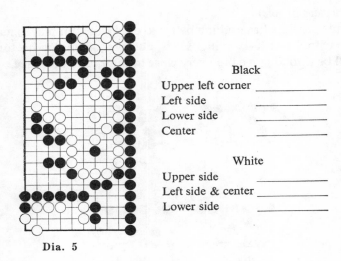

Dia. 5

Black	
Upper left corner	_____
Left side	_____
Lower side	_____
Center	_____

White	
Upper side	_____
Left side & center	_____
Lower side	_____

Dia. 6. These are the correct answers. We have not tried to suggest the order they should be played in, but started each separately with the number 1. Note that White will have to connect at 'a'. On the left edge, the marked black and white stones are the standard assumption to make for counting purposes.

If this were part of an actual game, quite possibly the board would look exactly like this in the end, although White might be able to get one of Black's *sente* endgame plays, or vice-versa.

Dia. 7. In the lower left corner Black could reduce White's corner by one more point if he started with 1 here, but he would end in *gote* instead of *sente*. One point is not likely to be worth the loss of a move.

Dia. 8. On the left side, if the marked stones have been played before Black plays 1, White should answer at 2. This may be worth one point to him, since it prevents Black 'a'.

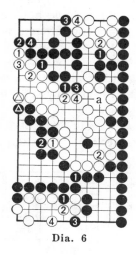

Dia. 6

Black
Upper left corner 12
Left side 16
Lower side 10
Center 1

White
Upper side 2
Left side & center 20
Lower side 5

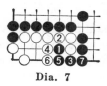

Dia. 7

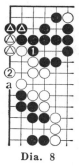

Dia. 8

There are two attitudes to be taken with regard to the timing of *sente*-endgame plays. On the one hand, you should make them as early in the game as possible — as soon as they actually become *sente* — lest the opportunity somehow get lost later. On the other hand, you should postpone then until the last possible moment — until just before your opponent is ready to take them from you — because you may want to use them as *ko* threats. Anyway, it is a bad idea to reduce your options unnecessarily. The second viewpoint is the correct one, although the first one has a certain amount of truth in it.

To see why *sente*-endgame plays should not generally be made too soon, consider the next three diagrams.

Dia. 9. In this joseki position, White has a large *sente*-endgame play at 1. He could take it even as early as the opening, but he should hold off until he is sure that he is not going to want to do something different with his stone.

Dia. 10. For example, he might want to play 1 here and start a running fight. This move would not be worth much after the exchange of *Dia. 9*.

Dia. 11. Or he might have a chance to spring the *tesuji* of 1 on his opponent. In this shape it threatens both a connection at 'a' and a play at 'b', which kills the marked black stones.

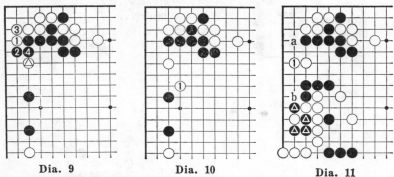

Dia. 9   Dia. 10   Dia. 11

c) Counting the Size of an Endgame Play

A different kind of counting is used to determine the size of individual plays, and to decide where the largest one is. You have to consider two things: the amount of profit to be gained, and the number of moves it takes to gain it. The following examples should show what we mean.

i) Double gote

Dia. 1. Black 1 is a large gote play. How much is it worth?

Dia. 2. When counting, you should assume that 1 here is Black's sente later.

Dia. 3. Compare the position in *Dia. 2* with this one, in which White has connected at 1 and can look forward to playing White 'a', Black 'b', White 'c', and Black 'd' later on. You will find that White's corner is six points larger and Black's territory five points smaller than before. That makes this an 11-point endgame situation, but both players must accept *gote* to get those 11 points.

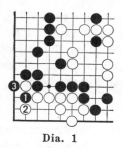
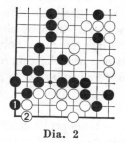
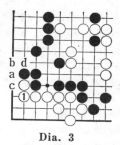

Dia. 1	Dia. 2	Dia. 3

ii) Reverse Endgame

Dia. 4. Black 1 is what is called a reverse-endgame play (*gyaku-yose* in Japanese). It is *gote*, but it keeps the opponent from making a *sente*-endgame play. After Black 1, the exchange of Black 'a' for White 'b' is reasonable to assume as a kind of *sente* endgame near the conclusion of the game.

Dia. 5. If White got to play 1 here, it would go like this. Compared with the last diagram, he has gained five points in *sente*.

Dia. 6. If Black tries to stop White 1 at 2, a *ko* fight occurs, with Black risking a big loss and White risking very little. It is hardly likely to be a good idea for Black to get into this unfavorable fight over only two points.

The opportunity to play reverse endgame arises more often than you might think, either through force of circumstance or because your opponent carelessly overlooks his own *sente*-endgame opportunities. How do reverse-endgame plays compare in importance with double-*gote* endgame plays?

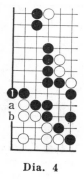
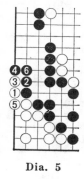

Dia. 4	Dia. 5	Dia. 6

Between *Dias.* 4 and 5, or in any other reverse-endgame situation, there is a difference of one play. In *Dia.* 5 Black and White have played the same number of stones, while in *Dia.* 4 Black has played one more than White. In a double-*gote* situation, however, there is always a difference of two plays. In *Dia.* 3, for instance, White has played one more stone than Black, while in *Dia.* 1 he has played one less. For this reason, x points in reverse endgame can be roughly considered to be worth 2x points in double-*gote*.

iii) Sente Endgame

Since any profit gained in *sente* is profit gained free, accurate counting is only necessary when there is some doubt as to whether the play is really going to be answered. For example —

Dia. 7. Black is thinking of playing 'a' and capturing a couple of stones, but if he does so, White will play 'b'. Black would like to play 'b' himself, have White answer at 'c', and then play 'a', but he has to consider the possibility that White will play 'd' instead of answering at 'c'. Which should he play then, 'a' or 'b'?

Dia. 8. If Black plays 1 and White does not answer, Black can follow with 3 and 5 in *sente*. (The words 'in *sente*' are an important part of the calculation). Later, 'a' is White's *sente*.

Dia. 9. Compare the last diagram with this one (again 'a' is White's *sente*), and you will see that White's territory is six points larger, and Black's four points smaller, than before. In other words, as a double-*gote* play, Black 1 in *Dia. 8* is worth ten points.

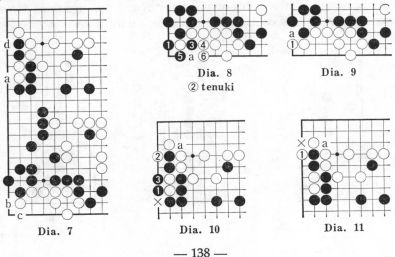

Dia. 8
② tenuki

Dia. 9

Dia. 7

Dia. 10

Dia. 11

Dia. 10. Black 1 here enlarges Black's territory by five points (two prisoners and the point x), and puts pressure on the cutting point at 'a'. At the very least, White will eventually have to play one more stone inside his territory to defend 'a'.

Dia. 11. White 1 enlarges White's territory by five points, (two prisoners and the point x), and now 'a' has ceased to be a cutting point at all. This double-*gote* play is worth at least eleven points.

In *Dia. 7*, therefore, it would be at least one point better for Black to play 'a', letting White have reverse endgame at 'b', than for him to play 'b' and let White get the two stones in the upper left.

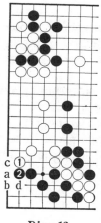

Dia. 12

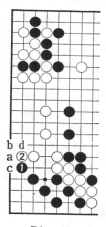

Dia. 13

iv) Double Sente

Dia. 12. White 1 can be considered a *sente*-endgame play, since it threatens a jump into Black's corner at 'd'. Black defends with 2, but White 'a', Black 'b', White 'c' and Black 'd' can be expected later.

Dia. 13. Black 1 here is also *sente*, and later the 'a' to 'd' exchange will also be his *sente*.

Comparing *Dias. 12* and *13*, you will see that whoever plays 1 enlarges his own territory by three points and reduces his opponent's territory by a like amount while keeping *sente*. Black and White have played one stone each in these diagrams, but there is a six-point difference between them.

Double-*sente* situations like these are of critical importance in the endgame. Both players should be on the lookout for the earliest possible chance to play 1 in *Dia. 12* or *13*. This is not at all like one-side *sente*-endgame moves, where the player who has the *sente* option can and should take his time about exercising it.

v) Ko

Dia. 14. Black has played 1 and 3 in what looks like a double-*sente* situation. However, White should pause for a moment before connecting at 'a'.

Dia. 15. If he lets Black cut there, he can still make *ko* with 2. Considering this, how much is a white (or black) play at 1 really worth?

In trying to estimate the value of such *ko* situations, the essential thing to do is to take stock of the *ko* threats available to both sides. If White is well ahead in *ko* material, he can allow *Dia. 15* and still save his corner with only a relatively small loss somewhere else.

But if Black is able to win the ko fight, he will gain _____ points. (You do the counting. You can get a very close estimate by counting two for every stone or unoccupied point involved, then subtracting three, but see if you can get the exact value.)

Ko threats are the most important things to consider, but beyond them, you should keep in mind that there is a three-play difference between White's winning, or preventing, the ko, and black's winning it, making ko an even slower way to gain profit than double-gote plays. In some kinds of *ko* fights, the difference between winning and losing is four plays or more.

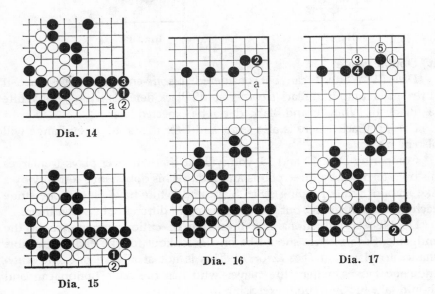

Dia. 14

Dia. 15

Dia. 16

Dia. 17

Dia. 16. Here, for example, White seems to be too cautious in preventing the *ko.* Black can play 2, a very large defensive move which threatens a further capture at 'a'.

Dia. 17. Better for White to play 1. If Black cuts at 2, White can follow with 3 and 5. There are several ways for Black to answer 5, but whatever he does, he will suffer a great setback in the upper right corner, as compared with *Dia. 16,* and the 29 points in the lower right corner are not his for certain until he plays another stone there.

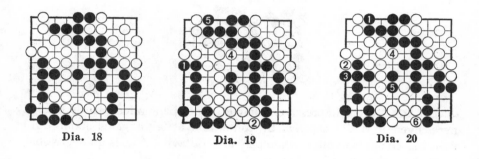

Dia. 18   Dia. 19   Dia. 20

vi) Dead-end plays and open-ended plays

Dia. 18 (Black to play)

In this artificial situation on a ten-by-ten board, there are five endgame plays left, each worth apparently one point. Which should Black take first, or doesn't it matter?

Dia. 19 (Correct)

There is no mystery about this problem. Black should play 1, and then he and White will split the remaining four endgame plays, two apiece. Black wins the game, 14 to 13.

Dia. 20 (Game ends in a draw)

What if Black starts elsewhere, allowing White to play 2? The best he can do is to answer at 3, but now White gains one more point than before, and the game ends in a draw.

Dia. 21 (Black loses)

If Black makes a policy of ignoring White's thrusts down the left side, until forced to answer at 7 to live, he will lose the game, 13 to 12.

There is a general principle lurking in this simple example, namely that open-ended plays like White 2 in *Dias. 20* and *21*, which not only take profit but also aim at further profit (or plays like Black 1 in *Dia. 19*, which prevent the former), are more valuable than plays like 2 to 5 in *Dia. 19*, which are dead-end gote.

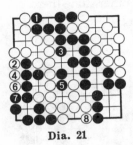

Dia. 21

Dia. 22. A more impressive example of an open-ended play is Black 1 here. Even if White answers by connecting at 'a', it gains about eight points as compared with a white play at 1. But what if, as is quite possible, White has other things to do than connect at 'a'?

Dia. 23. Next Black can gain further profit by capturing a stone with 1 and 3. After this, he can gain still more profit by playing 'a' (White answers at 'b'). Moreover, he can play 'b' himself and ruin White's eye shape at the side of the board. Because of this threat he can, for example, play 'c' in *sente*, perhaps getting a large territory in the center.

It is impossible to assign an exact numerical value to Black 1 in *Dia. 22*. All that can be said is that it is so large as to be almost a middle-game play rather than an endgame play.

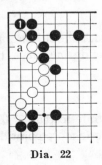

Dia. 22

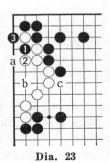

Dia. 23

d) Endgame Tesujis

This section is about *tesujis* in the endgame. The format is similar to Chapter Five, giving examples of each type of *tesuji*. In the concluding section, we give nine problems on small-size boards, so that you will gain some practice in co-ordinating the use of these *tesujis* in a game.

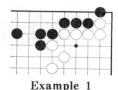

Example 1

1) The Throw-In Tesuji

Example 1

How can White gain one point in *sente*?

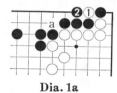

Dia. 1a

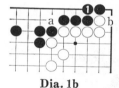

Dia. 1b

Dia. 1a. White throws in a stone at 1 and Black captures with 2. Eventually, Black will have to connect at 'a', losing one point. Compare this with the next diagram. where Black plays at 1.

Dia. 1b. If Black connects at 1, he doesn't have to play at 'a'. Moreover, he might have a chance to play at 'b' for additional profit.

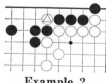

Example 2

Example 2

This position is almost the same as *Example 1*, except that White has played the marked stone. Is White's *tesuji* the same as before?

— 143 —

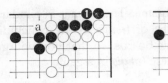
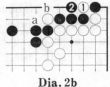
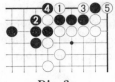

Dia. 2a   Dia. 2b   Dia. 2c

Dia. 2a. If Black connects at 1, this is the same as *Dia. 1b*, except that Black will eventually have to make another move at 'a'.

Dia. 2b. As before, if White throws in a stone at 1, it will be worth one more point, since Black must play at both 'a' and 'b'. However, White has a better way.

Dia. 2c. White should first hane at 1. Black must answer with 2 and the result after White 5 is more than two points better than *Dia. 2b*.

Dia. 2d. If Black connects with 2, White will play 3. Now Black 4 is forced. The sequence continues until Black captures four stones with 10, but amazingly White *ataris* at the point where the marked stone was (the under-the-stones *tesuji*) and catches six black stones.

Dia. 2d

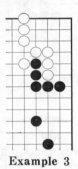

Example 3

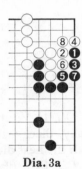

Dia. 3a

2) The Monkey Jump

Example 3

How can Black reduce White's corner?

Dia. 3a. Black should play the large-knight jump to 1. This move is known as the 'monkey jump'. The sequence continues to White 8 and Black ends in sente.

Dia. 3b. If White plays at 1, playing 3 and 5 later becomes his privilege, since Black ends in *gote*. Confirm for yourself that Black 1 in *Dia. 3a* is worth nine points in *sente* by comparing these two diagrams.

— 144 —

Example 4

This example is almost the same as before, but there is a slight difference. Black wants to reduce White's corner and still keep *sente*. Pay attention to the marked white stone.

Dia. 4a. If Black plays the monkey jump as in *Dia. 3a*, he will end in *gote* because of the presence of the marked white stone.

Dia. 4b. In this case, the small-knight move of Black 1 is the *tesuji*, enabling Black to keep *sente*. However, Black must settle for a smaller profit of only six points.

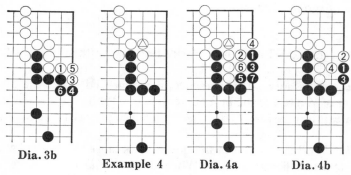

Dia. 3b   Example 4   Dia. 4a   Dia. 4b

Example 5

It is bad for White to exchange the marked stones. Black can now make big inroads into White's territory.

Dia. 5a. Black should attach with 1. After the sequence to White 8, Black ends in sente.

Dia. 5b. However, if Black plays the monkey jump to 1, his gain will be two points less than in *Dia. 5a*.

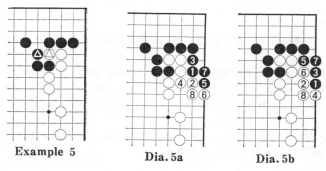

Example 5   Dia. 5a   Dia. 5b

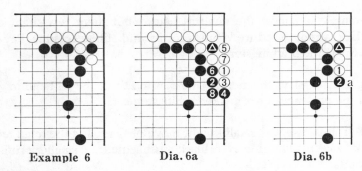

| Example 6 | Dia. 6a | Dia. 6b |

3) The Diagonal Extension

Example 6

How should White reduce Black's territory on the right side?

Dia. 6a. Because of the presence of the marked stone, the diagonal extension of White 1 is the best move. Up to 8, White has gained four points in sente. If it were Black's turn, he would also play at 1 (see *Example 22*).

Dia. 6b. White 1 is out of the question, because the marked stone leaves Black short of liberties. Now, White does not have the move at 'a' as a follow-up.

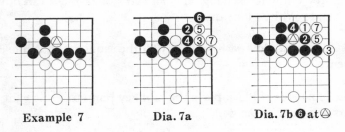

| Example 7 | Dia. 7a | Dia. 7b ❻ at △ |

Example 7

How should White utilize his marked stone?

Dia. 7a. White can take the corner away from Black with the moves to 7. Note that Black 2 (and not 3) is the vital point. If Black plays 2 at 3, White will attach at 5. However, White has a better way.

Dia. 7b. The diagonal extension of White 1 is the best move. It is at least eight points better for White than *Dia. 7a*.

Example 8

White wants to seal off his area at the top, but he must be careful, since his stones in the corner are not yet secure. What is White's best move?

Dia. 8a. Most players would simply block at 1. However, after exchanging 2 for 3, Black plays 4, and when White takes with 5, Black plays at 6. Now the white group in the corner doesn't have two eyes, and a *ko* results when Black plays 8. This will be a hard *ko* for White to win.

Dia. 8b. White must answer Black 2 with 3. After White 7, Black has made a deep intrusion into White's territory, while retaining *sente* .

Dia. 8c. The diagonal extension of 1 is White's best move. Black can only play at 2, which White easily counters by blocking at 3.

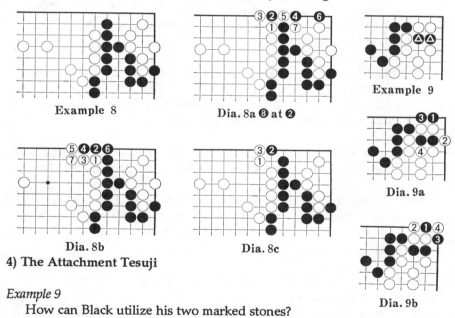

Example 8

Dia. 8a ❽ at ❷

Example 9

Dia. 9a

Dia. 8b

4) The Attachment Tesuji

Dia. 8c

Dia. 9b

Example 9

How can Black utilize his two marked stones?

Dia. 9a. The attachment of 1 forces White to take the two black stones with 2 and 4. If Black neglects to play at 1, then White should play at 3.

Dia. 9b. If White resists by blocking at 2, Black will play at 3. After White captures with 4, the fate of the corner hinges on a *ko*. This would be a wonderful result for Black.

Example 10
　How should Black play?

Dia. 10a. The moves to 8 might seem skillful, but Black has a better way.

Dia. 10b. Clamping at Black 1 is the *tesuji*. The sequence to Black 7 naturally follows. After this, Black can gain three more points in *sente* by playing at 'a'. This diagram is eight points better than *Dia. 10a*.

Example 11
　How should White reduce Black's territory?

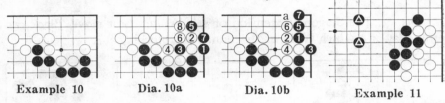

Example 10　　　Dia. 10a　　　　Dia. 10b　　　　Example 11

Dia. 11a. Clamping at White 1 forces Black to block at 2. After exchanging 3 for 4, White connects at 5 in *gote*. Later, White can play 7 and 9 in *sente* for an additional four points. Against White 7, Black cannot block at 9 because White would cut at 8, resulting in a *ko*.

Dia. 11b. If White connects at 5, the sequence to 10 would result in only a two-point gain for Black as opposed to a four-point gain in *Dia. 11a*.

Dia. 11c. Against White 1, Black could resist with 2, but when White descends to 7, Black must play 8, ending in *gote*. If he omits this move, White will play at 8, and the sequence from Black 'a' to 'g' will be worth seven points in *sente* for White.

Dia. 11d. Cutting at 1 looks tempting, but, because of the marked stone, White loses his stones after 12. If the marked stone were at 'a' or 'b', the cut at 1 would succeed. In that case, Black would answer by playing 4 at 5.

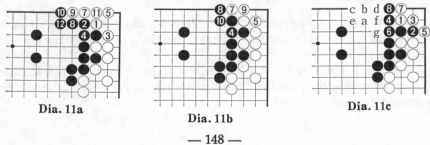

Dia. 11a　　　　　　Dia. 11b　　　　　　　Dia. 11c

5) Descending

Example 12
How should Black expand his corner territory?

Dia. 12a. Descending to 1 is the correct move. Next, Black 'a' is *sente*, so he can play here anytime he wants.

Dia. 12b. The *hane* of Black 1 is a mistake. White throws in a stone at 2, so Black must play at 'a' before he can connect at 2. In the meantime, White can fight a *ko*. This is better for White than *Dia. 12a.*

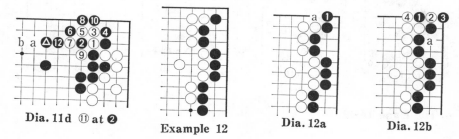

Dia. 11d ⑪ at ❷

Example 12

Dia. 12a

Dia. 12b

Example 13
How should Black play?

Dia. 13a. Descending to Black 1 is the *tesuji*. Later, Black can attach at 3; because of the cutting point at 'a', White ends in *gote* with 4 and 6.

Dia. 13b. Black 1 and 3 are bad moves. Black ends in *gote* without any follow-up.

Example 14
White has just played the marked stone. How should Black respond?

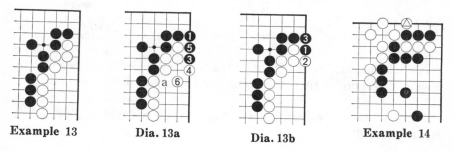

Example 13

Dia. 13a

Dia. 13b

Example 14

Dia. 14a. Turning at 2 is the vital point. What will happen if Black doesn't play this move?

Dia. 14b. If Black doesn't answer 1, then White will attach at 3, forcing Black to capture with 4 and 6. This gains White another three points. For Black to play at 1 is worth four points, so Black should take this point if White doesn't. Later, Black could play 'a' in *sente*.

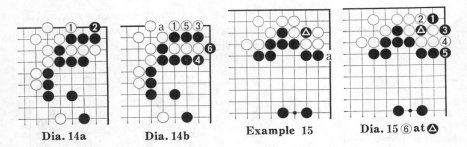

| Dia. 14a | Dia. 14b | Example 15 | Dia. 15 ⑥ at ▲ |

6) The Hane Tesuji

Example 15
White is threatening to *hane* at 'a' and gain two points, but there is still some life left in the marked black stone. How should Black to utilize this stone to prevent White 'a'?

Dia. 15. The *hane* of Black 1 is the correct move. Black takes *sente* when he plays 5, since White must connect at 6. Instead of 1, it would also be possible for Black to descend to 5, but it might not be *sente*.

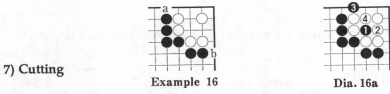

| Example 16 | Dia. 16a |

7) Cutting

Example 16
White is threatening to *hane* at 'a' and 'b'. However, Black has a way to prevent at least one of these threats and end in *sente*.

Dia. 16a. The cut at Black 1 forces White to respond with 2. Next, Black *hanes* at 3 in *sente*.

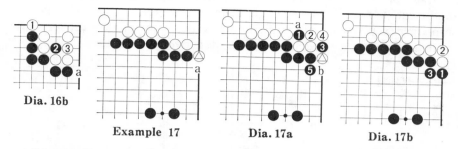

Dia. 16b   Example 17   Dia. 17a   Dia. 17b

Dia. 16b. If White gets to *hane* with 1, the cut of Black 2 has no meaning. After 3, Black must still defend against White 1, so he ends in *gote*. White next threatens to *hane* at 'a', again in *sente*.

Example 17

White has just played a *hane* with the marked stone. Blocking at 'a' seems to be the commonsense move. However, Black has a better way which will reduce White's area by at least one point.

Dia. 17a. The cut of Black 1 is the correct way to answer the marked white stone. White 2 is forced. Black throws in a stone at 3, then extends to 5. Black now threatens to descend to 'a' in *sente* to gain another point, but if White captures at 'a', he will end in *gote*. Moreover, if Black can play at 'a', the point 'b' will become his.

Dia. 17b. Clearly, Black 1 and 3 in this diagram are inferior compared to *Dia. 17a.* In both cases, Black ends in *gote*, but *gote* in *Dia. 17a* is one to two points better for Black than here.

Example 18

Where is Black's endgame *tesuji* ?

Dia. 18a. Black should first cut at 1. White must answer with 2, and the sequence continues to White 8. Black can play at 9 any time he chooses.

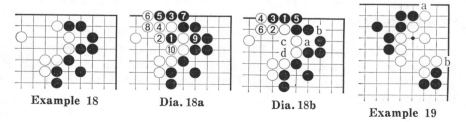

Example 18   Dia. 18a   Dia. 18b   Example 19

Dia. 18b. If Black unthinkingly *hanes* with 1 and continues up to White 6, the cut at 'c' becomes meaningless, since White can answer at 'd'. White can now play 'a' in sente any time he wants, since Black must respond with 'b'. Confirm for yourself that *Dia. 18a* is two points better.

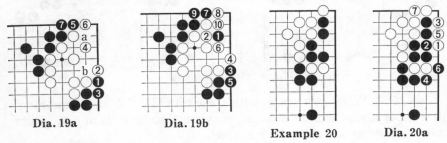

| Dia. 19a | Dia. 19b | Example 20 | Dia. 20a |

8) The Placement Tesuji

Example 19

Black wants to *hane* at both 'a' and 'b' and end in sente. How can he do this?

Dia. 19a. If Black carelessly *hanes* at 1, after Black 3, White will play at 4. Now when Black plays at 7, White can play elsewhere, as his stone at 4 defends both points 'a' and 'b'.

Dia. 19b. The placement of Black 1 is the *tesuji*. After White connects at 2, Black can play the sequence to 9 in *sente,* since White must connect at 10. If White plays 2 at 10, Black will *atari* at 2. Now where is Black's tesuji? (Hint: see Example 9.)

Example 20

Where is White's *tesuji*?

Dia. 20a. The placement of White 1 is the *tesuji*. After Black connects with 2, White forces with 3 and 5, then finally connects with 7.

Dia. 20b. The *hane* of 1 fails, since Black can now play 2. The marked white stones no longer have any effect on the corner.

Dia. 20c. The atari of White 1 is also bad. When Black plays 6, White can't play at 'a' because he is short of liberties. However, Black will be able to play at 'a' any time he chooses. This diagram is two points better for Black than *Dia. 20a.*

Example 21

This position results from the *joseki* shown in the reference diagram. Where should Black play?

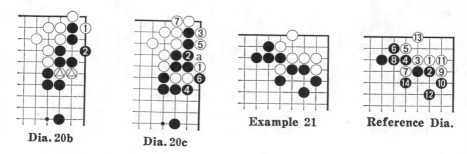

Dia. 20b Dia. 20c Example 21 Reference Dia.

Dia. 21a. The placement of Black 1 is the *tesuji*. After White 2, Black descends to 3, then throws in a stone with 5. White can't play at 7 because he is short of liberties. Instead, he must take one stone with 6, so Black will then take a stone with 7. This pattern comes up so often that it is worth learning by heart.

Dia. 21b. If Black simply descends with 1, White will take the vital point of 2. Now all Black can do is *atari* with 3. The sequence in *Dia. 21a* is three points better. However, Black ends in *gote*, so proper timing is important.

Example 22

How should Black defend his territory at the top?

Dia. 22a. The *atari* of Black 1 is bad. If Black plays elsewhere after 2, White can play 4 and 6, ending in sente. Black must play 5 instead of blocking at 6, because White is threatening to play a *ko*.

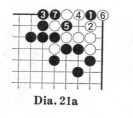

Dia. 21a

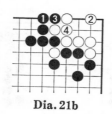

Dia. 21b

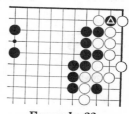

Example 22

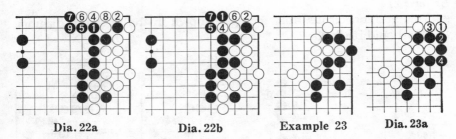

| Dia. 22a | Dia. 22b | Example 23 | Dia. 23a |

Dia. 22b. Black 1 is the *tesuji.* White must capture with 2, so now Black can play elsewhere. Later, the best intrusion White can make into Black's territory is with 4 and 6. This is two points better for Black than *Dia. 22a.*

Example 23

This example is similar to *Example 22.* Where should White play?

Dia. 23a. Again the placement of White 1 is the *tesuji.* After Black connects at 4, White has taken the corner in *sente.*

Dia. 23b. If White *ataris* with 1, Black will *hane* with 2. Next, when White takes two stones with 3, Black will recapture at the marked stone with 4. This is at least one point worse for White than *Dia. 23a.*

Example 24

What is the best way for Black to save his two marked stones?

Dia. 24a. Jumping to Black 1 is best. If White pushes through with 2, Black will connect at 3. White will play 4 elsewhere (as Black wouldn't answer White 5), so Black can later play 5 and 7 in *sente.*

Dia. 24b. If White blocks at 2 in answer to 1, then Black will simply connect at 3. There is no difference in the score between this diagram and *Dia. 24a.*

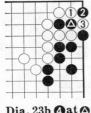

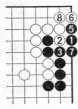

| Dia. 23b ❹at ▲ | Example 24 | Dia. 24a | Dia. 24b |

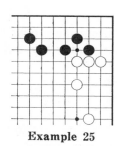

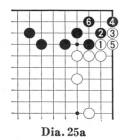

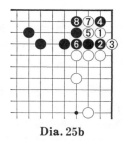

| Example 25 | Dia. 25a | Dia. 25b |

Example 25

White wants to reduce Black's corner territory. Where is the best move?

Dia. 25a. The moves in this diagram are artless. White has a much better move.

Dia. 25b. Jumping to White 1 is the *tesuji*. It is useless for Black to resist with the moves to 8.

Dia. 25c. In answer to White 1, Black's best defense is to play at 2. However, White can still take the corner with the sequence up to 7.

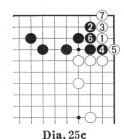

Dia. 25c

e) Endgame Problems

In a game a player is faced with not just one local endgame problem but with many interconnected ones, with *sente* and *gote* relationships between them. Calculating the value of each move is not enough. In this section, we will present nine problems in order to give the reader some experience in coordinating many endgame positions throughout the board.

These problems range from the very easy to difficult. The first four problems are direct applications of what has been learned in the preceding section. The remaining problems are more difficult and will be a challenge even to strong players.

The reader should try to solve these problems before looking at the answers. In this way, he will develop his power to read out endgame positions when confronted by them in his games. The solutions to these problems require finding the best moves for both players, the order in which they should be played, and the final scoring.

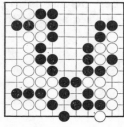

Problem 1

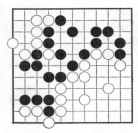

Problem 2

Problem 1
   Black to play. Where are the biggest endgame moves?

Problem 2
   What are the best endgame moves if Black plays first?

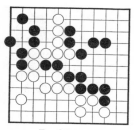

Problem 3

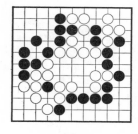

Problem 4

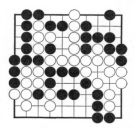

Problem 5

Problem 3
Black to play. What is the best endgame sequence?

Problem 4
Black to play. How must Black play to win the game?

Problem 5
White to play and win. Find the best moves for both sides.

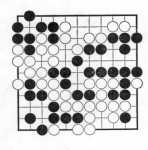

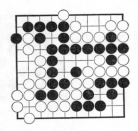

Problem 6

Problem 7

Problem 6
   White to play. What are the best moves for both?

Problem 7
   If Black plays correctly, he will win by one point.

Problem 8
   Black to play and get a draw.

Problem 9
   Black to play and get a draw.

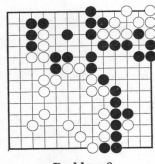

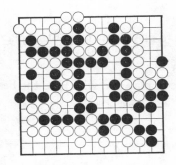

Problem 8

Problem 9

Answers to Endgame Problems

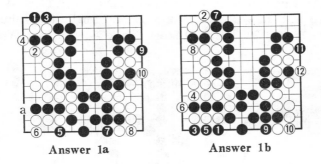

Answer 1a   Answer 1b

Answer 1a

Attaching at 1, forcing White to capture two stones with 2 and 4, is Black's biggest endgame play. Next, Black hanes with 5 and White answers by descending at 6. Finally Black 7 and 9 are *sente* and the game is now over. Eventually White will have to play another stone at 'a', so in the final count White has 28 points and Black has 29. Black wins by one point.

Answer 1b

If Black hanes at 1 here instead of attaching at 1 in *Ans. 1a*, the moves to White 12 will follow. The final result is a draw.

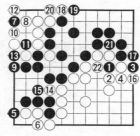

Answer 2

Answer 2

The cut of Black 1 is an endgame *tesuji* we studied a few pages back. White must answer with 2 and 4. Black then plays another big endgame move at 5 in *sente*. After White connects at 6, Black places a stone at 7 and gains another three points in *gote* with the moves to 13. Next, White plays his last two *sente* moves with 14 and 16, and finally takes the last two points with 18 and 20. The final score: Black — 30 points; White — 29 points.

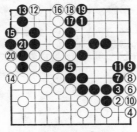

Answer 3

Answer 3

Black's first priority is to defend his territory at the top right without endangering his stones at the top left. The diagonal extension of Black 1 is the endgame *tesuji*. Next, White *hanes* at 2 and makes an open connection at 4. Black 5 is worth five points in *gote*. Next, White plays 6. Black must submissively answer at 7. If Black blocks at 8 with 7, White will cut at 7 and a *ko* will result. Black ends in gote when he connects at 11, and White has gained four points in *sente*. Finally, White plays a series of *sente* moves with 12 to 20. Note that Black must answer 14 with 15. The final score is 28 points for Black and 27 for White.

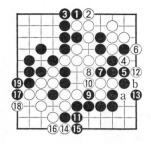

Answer 4

Answer 4

Even though they are worth only three points in *gote*, Black 1 and 3 are the biggest endgame moves. The points 4 and 11 are, of course, bigger, but since there are two of them, if White takes one, Black will take the other. Therefore, they balance each other out. It would be a four-point difference in the final score if Black didn't play here, because a white move at 3 would be *sente*. A white move at 4 is one point better than one at 11. After White 6, Black plays 7 and 9 in *sente*, then takes the big endgame point at 11, which is worth six points. White 12 and Black 13 are the last real points. White 14 and 16, and Black 17 and 19 are of equal value. For this reason, if Black had answered White 12 at 'a', White would have played at 'b' and gained another point. This result is a draw: each side has 31 points.

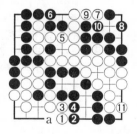

Answer 5

Answer 5

White 1 and 3 are *sente*, since they threaten to kill the black group at the bottom. (If White first plays 1 at 5, Black will play at 3, White 6, Black 'a' in *sente*. Next, Black would play at 9 and win the game.) After Black secures his stones at the bottom with 4, White 5 is the next biggest move. Connecting at 6 is worth five points. Attaching at 7 is White's last *tesuji*, worth three points in sente. (Do you see why Black can't play 8 at 10?) After Black 10, White takes the last point of value with 11. The final score is: Black — 12 points; White — 14 points.

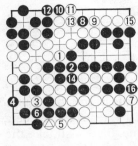

Answer 6

Answer 7

⑲ at ❸ ㉒ at △ ㉕ at ❸
㉘ at △ ㉛ at ❸

Answer 6

White 1 threatens to take 12 points in profit by playing at 2. After Black defends at 2, White cuts at 3. Black must defend with 4, so White can now save his marked stone in *sente* with 5. Next, descending to 7 is White's biggest point, taking at least a six-point profit in *gote*. Now it's Black's turn to play a *tesuji*. He attaches at 8 and White must respond with 9. Next, Black 10 and 12 become *sente*. Black now connects at 14, saving two stones for a profit of four points. Finally, White 15 (worth 2 1/2 points) and Black 16 (worth 2 points) are the last points of the game. The result is a draw, 18 points for each side.

Answer 7

Black cuts at 1 and throws in a stone at 3. The meaning of these moves will become clear in a moment. Next, Black sacrifices a stone with 5. This is worth one point in *sente* for Black. Black now defends at 9. (If not, White could play at 9 himself in *sente*, aiming at 20.) White 10 and 12 deprive Black of three points. After exchanging 13 for 14, Black plays 15, forcing White to capture with 16. (If White connects at 3, Black will throw in a stone at 29 and White can't capture because he is short of liberties. Black 17 deprives White of a *ko* threat and after White 18, Black starts a *ko* with 19. Finally, after Black takes the *ko* with 31, White runs out of *ko* threats. Black wins by one point, having 15 points against White's 14. You should note that Black won this endgame by skillfully preparing for the *ko* fight.

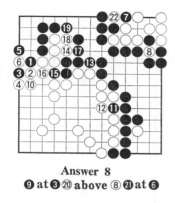

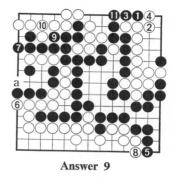

Answer 8

Answer 9

9 at **3** **20** above **8** **21** at **6**

Answer 8

Because of the double *ko* in the upper right corner, Black has an infinite number of *ko* threats. Therefore, Black can win any *ko*. Black begins by playing 1 and 3. When White blocks with 4, Black makes an open connection with 5, creating a *ko*. After White takes with 6, Black makes a *ko* threat with 7. White must answer by taking with 8, and Black takes the *ko* by recapturing with 9 at 3. White has no choice but to connect with 10. Black 11 is *sente* and Black 13 is the biggest *gote* move. The sequence up to Black 19 naturally follows. When White connects with 20 (at the point above 8), Black connects with 21 (at 6). After White 22, Black can't win the *ko* because White has more *ko* threats. The final result is a draw. Both Black and White have 48 points.

Answer 9

Black 1 is a hard move to see. Even many strong players would choose to descend at 11 with 1, threatening to play 1. However, this would give White the chance to play at 9. Black 1 and 3 are high-level probing moves that aim to set up a *ko* in the right corner by using the threat of playing at 11 should White block at 3 with 2. Therefore, White must submissively play 2 and 4. Next, Black plays 5, leaving the situation in the upper right corner for the time being. White 6 is *sente*, since he threatens to play at 'a'. Black 7 is the best defense; any other way would lose a point. Next, White goes back to defend at 8 and Black plays at 9 to take another point before connecting at 11. This sequence is the only way Black can get a draw. The final score is 32 points each.

Appendix

This appendix was added to update the *joseki* discussed in *Dia.* 2 on page 64. The following analysis and problems are due to Rob van Zeijst.

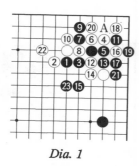

Dia. 1

Dia. 2

Dia. 1 (New joseki)

These days, after White 6, Black often plays 7. After Black's severe move at 9, there are three main variations. White 10 is the most common response. A complicated fight will ensue in which the corner changes hands several times. White's cut at 12 seems to put Black on the spot, but the combination of Black 13 and 15 save the situation. In exchange, White recaptures the corner. Sometimes White omits 22, because it is not absolutely *sente*, and even if Black answers at 23 (usually a wise decision), it may just turn out that this move will deny Black some options that he might have had if this move weren't made.

Dia. 2 (Special strategy)

White 4 is a special strategy. It aims to attack the black stones in the center, which are somewhat weak, but the profit Black gains in the corner is quite large, without any weaknesses, and White does not have any territory to speak of. Moreover, Black can lay waste to any territory White might make at the top by jumping to 'e'. Playing Black 'b', White 'c', and Black 'd' is a reasonable follow-up. Black 9 is a tricky move to spot, for the natural move would be A. Problem 1 on page 166 reveals White's hidden intentions.

Dia. 3 (Goose pimples)

This is the kind of situation in which a go player discovers that goose-pimples are not a physical sensation experienced only in winter. It is hard to tell if Black is being subtle or crude by playing the sequence 5 to 13. Black's ace-in-the-hole is his abundance of *ko* threats. White 18 and 20 are the best moves White can come up with. Instead of 18, White could connect at 5. In that case Black *ataris* at A, White takes the *ko*, and Black plays B as his ko threat. After this, White has no choice but to submit by playing at 18 and 20 after all.

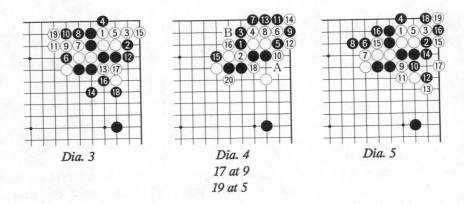

Dia. 3

Dia. 4

17 at 9

19 at 5

Dia. 5

Dia. 4 (Bad moves)

Black must avoid moves like 6, etc. The moves to 12 are natural, but White then cuts at 13 and Black finds himself short of liberties if he now tries to save his stones in the center with 14, for example, After 15 White dan either capture the black stones at the top or the four in the corner. This is exactly the kind of result that White wants.

Dia. 5 (Ko)

In this diagram, Black is a bit too kind to himself. White could also cut at 14 instead of 9. This may be good enough, but just in case White goes for everything . . . The resulting *ko* is the best Black can do. In the problem section some details about individual moves are discussed. Success!

Three Problems

Problem 1. Instead of playing A, the joseki move, Black decides to avoid bad shape and ventures at 1. White to move and capture the two marked stones.

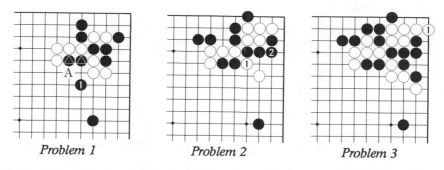

Problem 1   Problem 2   Problem 3

Problem 2. This is a problem based on *Dia. 5*. After White 9 in *Dia. 5* (White 1 in this diagram), Black connects at 2, apparently in an attempt to win liberties. White to capture the Black stones.

Problem 3. White tries to be clever. (Remember: a move is only tesuji as long as it works.) How does Black take advantage of the situation?

Answer

Answer 1a. White first descends to 1, after which Black has to defend the corner with 2. Next, White sets up a loose ladder and catches the Black stones with the moves to 13.

Answer 1b. Black offers more resistance by playing at 2 here, but White 7 is an exquisite tesuji threatening to capture the black stones in the corner and those in the center. If Black defends the corner with 8, White 9 and 11 seal the fate of the Black's center stones. In the odd case that Black does not defend the corner, White throws in at A, Black captures at B, White C, Black A, and White ataris at D, capturing Black's stones on his next move.

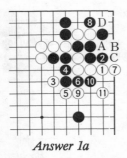

Answer 1a

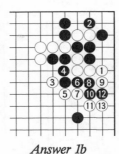

Answer 1b

Answer 2. After Black 1. White first forces 2 for 3 to create a shortage of liberties for Black and then starts filling in liberties. White 6, by the way, creates an extra liberty. In the sequence to 10, White wins the capturing race.

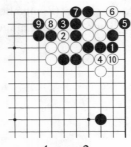

Answer 2

Answer 3. Cutting at 1 is only natural. White 2 aims at throwing in at 3. Black follows the principle: 'Play at the point where you opponent wants to play,' and after White 4, with the sequence to 9, Black will either set up a ladder or will simply capture the marked stones.

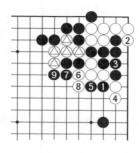

Answer 3

Keep in mind that you will never find the situation in Problems 2 and 3 on your board (at least not when you are playing Black), because you now know how to avoid them.

Go Books from Ishi Press

Beginner Books

AN INTRODUCTION TO GO
James Davies and Richard Bozulich

THE MAGIC OF GO
by Cho Chikun

THE WORLD OF GO
Anything you would ever want to know about Go

Elementary Books

THE SECOND BOOK OF GO
Richard Bozulich

BASIC TECHNIQUES OF GO
Haruyama Isamu and Nagahara Yoshiaki

TEST YOUR GO STRENGTH
Miyamoto Naoki

LESSONS IN THE FUNDAMENTALS OF GO
Kageyama Toshiro

Elementary Go Series

VOLUME 1: IN THE BEGINNING
Ishigure Ikuro

VOLUME 2: 38 BASIC JOSEKI
Kosugi Kiyoshi and James Davies

VOLUME 3: TESUJI
   James Davies

VOLUME 4: LIFE AND DEATH
   James Davies

VOLUME 5: ATTACK AND DEFENSE
   Ishida Akira and James Davies

VOLUME 6: THE ENDGAME
   Ogawa Tomoko and James Davies

VOLUME 7: HANDICAP GO
   Nagahara Yoshiaki and Richard Bozulich

Intermediate Books

STRATEGIC CONCEPTS OF GO
   Nagahara Yoshiaki

KAGE'S SECRET CHRONCLES OF HANDICAP GO
   Kageyama Toshiro

THE BREAKTHROUGH TO SHO-DAN
   Miyamoto Naoki
APPRECIATING FAMOUS GAMES
   Ohira Shuzo

KATO'S ATTACK AND KILL
   Kato Masao
THE POWER OF THE STAR-POINT
   Takagawa Shukaku

THE CHINESE-STYLE FUSEKI
   Kato Masao

ALL ABOUT THICKNESS
  Ishida Yoshio

THE 3–3 POINT
  Cho Chikun

POSITIONAL JUDGMENT
  Cho Chikun

Advanced Books

DICTIONARY OF BASIC JOSEKI (3 Volumes)
  Ishida Yoshio

Go-playing and shogi-playing software also available, as well as books on shogi (Japanese chess) and Chinese chess. Send for a free catalog of books, software, oriental game equipment and current price list.

In North America order from:
  Ishi Press International
  76 Bonaventure Drive
  San Jose, CA 94043
  Telephone: (408) 944-9900   FAX 408-944-9110

In Europe and U.K. order from:
  Ishi Press International, Ltd.
  20 Bruges Place, Baynes Street
  London NW1 0TE
  Telephone: 071-284-4898   FAX 071-284-4899

Other Countries:
  The Ishi Press, Inc.
  CPO Box 2126, Tokyo, Japan
  Telephone: 0467-83-4369 FAX 0467-83-4710
  VISA and Mastercard accepted.